Then the Sun Came Up

With a heart full of gratitude,
I dedicate this book
to the keen, attractive, modern-day women who
open Aigner bags to deal their bread to the hungry,
drive their wagons to help the afflicted,
recycle their Pendletons to clothe the naked,
tramp hospital and prison corridors to share the gospel;
to the women with fewer material possessions
who gratefully share all they have;
to the many wonderful women
who daily enact Isaiah 58:7;
and to the innumerable fine women
whom I love in Christ—
especially the Tuesday Morning Prayer Group
in Raleigh.

Then the Sun Came Up

by

Helen Polston Tucker

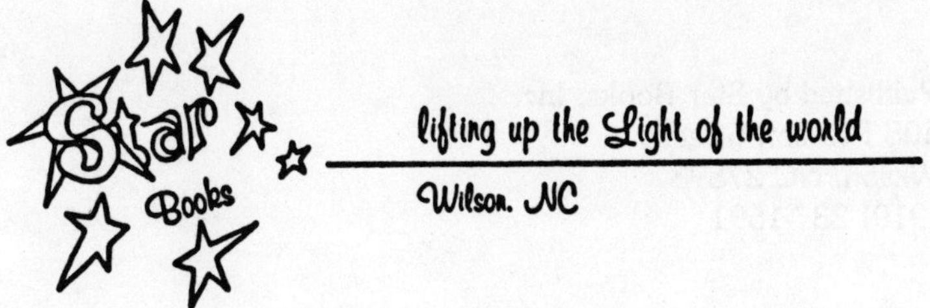

This is a true story, but some names have been changed to protect the privacy of individuals involved.
All Scriptures are quoted from the King James Version of the Bible unless otherwise identified.

ISBN 0-915541-10-6

Library of Congress Catalog Card Number: 86-060848

Published by Star Books, Inc.
408 Pearson Street
Wilson, NC 27893
(919) 237-1591

Contents

Preface ... vii
Foreword ... ix
1. The Holiday ... 1
2. Temporary Pleasures or Lasting Joy? ... 5
3. What Is the Matter with Me? ... 11
4. The Answer ... 17
5. Entrance to a Strange Land ... 25
6. Room 321 ... 31
7. The Holding Room ... 37
8. Is This Trip Absolutely Necessary? ... 41
9. Learning to Relax ... 45
10. The Unexpected Visitor ... 51
11. Walking—but Not Leaping ... 59
12. HPT Delivery Service ... 65
13. Patricia ... 71
14. "Where Will We Go Tomorrow?" ... 77
15. The Queen of the Nile ... 83
16. The Swing Shift ... 91
17. The Medicine of a Merry Heart ... 97
18. "Victory Day" ... 103
19. Going Home ... 111
20. Stormy Weather ... 117
21. Doctors, Friends, and Strangers ... 125
22. A Love Story ... 133
23. A Winter Weekend at the Beach ... 139
24. A Night on the Town ... 147
25. Coronation ... 153
26. Assignment from God ... 161
Appendix ... 167

Is not this the kind of fasting I have chosen:
to loose the chains of injustice
    and untie the cords of the yoke,
to set the oppressed free
    and break every yoke?
Is it not to share your food with the hungry
    and to provide the poor wanderer with shelter—
when you see the naked, to clothe him,
    and not to turn away from your own flesh and blood?
THEN YOUR LIGHT WILL BREAK FORTH LIKE THE DAWN,
    AND YOUR HEALING WILL QUICKLY APPEAR;
then your righteousness will go before you,
    and the glory of the Lord will be your rear guard.
Then you will call, and the Lord will answer;
    you will cry for help, and he will say: Here am I.

Isaiah 58:6-9a NIV

Preface

Some people feel that God must always deliver them out of trouble, and that if He doesn't, something is radically wrong with them—or even with Him.

I have found that He wants, always, to be "a very present help *in* trouble" (Psalm 46:1, italics added). There are times when His highest purpose can be achieved only as we walk with Him through the fiery furnace. His processes of dealing with me are more important and more desirable than my own desires. When I believe this, then I have victory even in the midst of trouble.

In presenting my story concerning these things, I would like to make the following acknowledgments:

First and foremost, I acknowledge Jesus Christ as my Lord and Savior and Healer of the whole person—body, soul, and spirit.

And I certainly acknowledge, also, that without the human help that He provided through

the loving hearts of the body of Christ,
the medical profession of Raleigh,
my talented editor, Catherine Jackson of Winston-Salem,
my God-appointed publisher, Irene Burk Harrell,
my loyal family throughout the state of North Carolina,
and most of all my best friend, my husband, Tuck,

I might never have lived to tell this story, and you might never have read it. So come, rejoice with me that you have been assured of a happy ending before you begin to laugh and cry your way through this journey to wholeness.

Foreword

One day my wife, the author of this book, said to me, "What famous person do we know who can write the Foreword for our book?"

"Well," I said, rubbing my chin thoughtfully, "one of my fraternity brothers at Chapel Hill married the daughter of a former president. . . . Will that do?"

"I don't think so," she said, shaking her head. "I believe you'd better write it; you know me better."

"What? Me? And ruin your book?" I protested. "You know it will sound just like an attorney's brief if I do it. Very dull."

"Better dull than a fraternity man's preamble to life in the White House," she argued. "You write it."

"We'll see," I said, noncommittally and somewhat doubtfully, as I rolled a piece of paper in her typewriter and began at the beginning. . . .

My wife was born in Raeford, NC. Two months after she graduated from high school, her family moved to Mullins, SC; three years later, they moved to Whiteville, NC. There the Lord put her in the house across the street from my family's home.

I knew when I saw the huge moving van pull out of our neighbor's driveway that the new girl standing on the sidewalk was going to make me a fine neighbor. She looked a little young, but I had hopes that looks were deceiving. Besides, I wanted to get acquainted right away, knowing that the Lord must have placed her right there, for me, on my very doorstep. I wouldn't disappoint Him.

We were married five months later. Two children later we moved to Raleigh, NC, so I could be an Assistant U.S. District Attorney.

At first, everything worked out fine; all His wonderful plans for us were being carried out. Helen and I were both born again in Whiteville and received the baptism in the Holy Spirit in Raleigh.

The trial of her faith—mine too—came with the birth of our only grandchild, who was born autistic. But the Lord moved into this potential catastrophe and turned it into a miracle. Helen and I joined with two other couples who had retarded children and founded the Tammy Lynn Foundation, which became an outstanding institution known all over the United States for its superb care and treatment of severely and profoundly retarded children.

Helen's Christianity was next put to the test through an operation for cancer, which had already claimed the lives of three members of her immediate family. Her experience with cancer is the focal point of this book, in which she leads us through her life as a child, a patient, and a growing Christian with humor and discernment. Her own personal journey through the wilderness is upbeat and encouraging, with the Lord Jesus as her constant companion.

Helen's Christianity is the real thing. I know. I was there. I watched as she and Jesus worked together, turning trying experiences into triumphs for the Lord. I know Helen better than any other living person knows her, and I have truly seen her laugh and praise God—and learn from Him—through all her pain, heartaches, and traumas. Few people are called upon to conquer as many varied difficulties as she has faced in her lifetime.

Afterward, I watched as the Lord sent her out to speak and encourage others at meetings, in prisons, hospitals, and tea parties throughout Eastern North Carolina, still rejoicing, still smiling. In the midst of all this, Helen has also free-lanced for newspapers and magazines, and has authored several as yet unpublished books of poetry and devotional books. As I see it, Helen's talents in writing seem to be increasingly fruitful for the Kingdom of God as she helps people who need the kind of love Jesus has given to her to share.

Yes, I remember vividly the New Year's Day when she found the lump as the two of us were watching the bowl game on the TV set in our motel room at Virginia Beach. We were concerned, of course, but I never believed it was cancerous—not until the Doctor informed me that it was. . . .

Looking back now, I can see that God had a plan. Although I don't believe that God afflicts anyone, I surely believe that He knows how to make afflictions turn out for our good and His glory as we give it all to Him, as Helen did and does. Now, I can see that God's plan is being fulfilled eight years later with the publication of this book to help His hurting children.

I am of the opinion that a reading of this book, *Then the Sun Came Up,* will uplift many. Here you will see the triumph of God's children over a circumstance that has devastated many who do not know Him. Reader, read on, and be blessed.

Irvin B. Tucker, Jr.
Raleigh, NC

1

The Holiday

This New Year's Eve would be different from any other I had ever spent with my husband.

Tuck and I had just arrived at the motel in Virginia Beach, Virginia, where we had made reservations for a weekend holiday. Just as we were getting out of our car, two police cars whizzed up beside us, hemming us in.

My husband and I watched, bewildered, as three policemen leaped from their squad cars and rushed past us into the motel office. What in the world was going on?

Hearing the screech of tires, we turned just in time to see a nearby car scratch off from the curb and make a hasty exit from the motel grounds. Tuck grabbed my arm and held it tightly. Immediately, the policemen ran out of the building, jumped into their patrol cars, and gave chase—sirens wailing, blue lights flashing. The scene resembled something from a TV drama.

"I never expected to be on the scene, in live action," I whispered to my husband as we huddled close together beside our car.

After the police left the parking lot, the small crowd that had gathered to watch the excitement began to disperse. The drama over, Tuck and I collected our wits and went to the motel office to register and ask what the excitement was all about. We were told that a robbery had occurred just in time for us to witness the getaway.

On the way to our room, Tuck and I discussed what had happened. Although we were somewhat shaken by our roles as innocent bystanders in the melodramatic scene, we were thankful that no one was hurt, and we made up our minds not to let the incident dampen our enthusiasm for our New Year's holiday. Nevertheless, it left me with a lingering feeling of apprehension. I tried to dismiss it from my mind. *We mustn't let anything spoil our time together,* I thought, as Tuck unlocked the door to our room.

"I'll unpack the bags later," I said. "Let's watch the game now."

Tuck turned on the television set, found the channel carrying the New Year's Eve bowl game, and settled in a chair to enjoy the first hours of our vacation. I plopped down on a bed, propping myself against the pillows, to watch with him. Since I had been secretly studying sports magazines for weeks in order to impress my husband with my knowledge of football, I now offered my professional opinions freely.

As I was demonstrating to Tuck how the quarterback could have improved his lateral pass, my arm swept across my breast. Something caused me to stop in mid-gesture. Was that a lump I felt? It *couldn't* be! Unobtrusively, I dropped my hand to my breast and felt the suspicious area with suddenly shaky fingers. There really *was* a lump!

Swallowing hard, I announced as calmly as possible, "I have just found a lump in my breast." Slowly, Tuck turned his head toward me, unbelief etched on his handsome features. Football forgotten now, he rose quickly from his chair, saying half-aloud, "Honey, no! You must be mistaken."

His voice trailed off into the air. Leaning over the bed, he gently touched my cheek with a trembling hand. As scared as I felt at the moment, my heart was moved with pity for him. "Yes, honey, there really is a lump," I told him gently. "I can feel it through my blouse."

Taking his hand in mine, I guided his fingers to the hard, unfamiliar lump. "Yes," he said reluctantly, "I feel it." Then he wrapped his arms around me, rocking me back and forth like a mother soothing her hurt child. I sensed that he was calling out to the Lord, but no words were spoken. We clung to each other for comfort.

When I began shivering, Tuck released me and rummaged in the dresser drawers until he found some blankets. I suppose it was shock that caused me to become suddenly chilled. I was thinking about the two members of my family who had died of cancer during my lifetime. *But this won't be cancer,* I assured myself.

My husband seemed calm as he wrapped the blankets around me, but the light had left his eyes. We didn't talk but sat close together in silence. I knew Tuck was praying, and I was reminding the Lord that He was my Life, my Hope, my Redeemer. As warmth returned to my body, there came to my racing mind something a missionary had said in a Bible class I had attended at least twenty-five years earlier. Nothing, she told us, can touch a Christian without first passing through the hand of God. The vivid recollection of those words brought me comfort. Through His hand? Then He must have some reason for allowing this to happen. *I don't have to understand it,* I reminded myself. *If I just trust, then I'm all right. Just relax. God is in charge. I know we can depend on His love, trust Him regardless.* I thought of His promise in Romans 8:28, "And we know that all things work together for good to them that love God . . . ," and then I felt better.

For the first time since my announcement, I spoke. "Tuck, I'd like to go home."

"Now?" he asked, holding me closer.

"No, but the first thing tomorrow."

Taking my hand, Tuck dropped to his knees beside the bed. As we prayed aloud and committed the problem to our Lord, both of us felt the assurance that God heard us and that He was absolutely in command of the whole situation.

If God is in command of your circumstances, what do you do on New Year's Eve? Celebrate, of course—and that's what we did, with a candlelight dinner and Jesus! We had a joyful evening and looked forward to the New Year together, knowing that Jesus is Lord over everything—including lumps.

As Tuck reached over to turn off the bedside lamp, he whispered into the darkness, "Happy 1978! It *will* be, honey." Putting his arm over me, he held me tight until he fell asleep.

dresser drawer. Later he found some pictures, I suppose, [illegible] that caused me to become suddenly chilled. [illegible] members of my family who had died or [illegible] during my [illegible]. But this wasn't the answer, I reasoned to myself.

My husband became calm as he wrapped [illegible] around me. [illegible] the light and [illegible]. We didn't talk but sat close together in silence. I knew Tuck was praying and I was reminded [illegible] that He was my [illegible] my Redeemer. As my mind returned [illegible] there came to my [illegible] mind [illegible] I had said in [illegible] class I had attended at least twenty-five years earlier. [illegible] passing through the hand of God. [illegible] Then He must have [illegible] for allowing this to happen? I don't have to understand [illegible] God is [illegible] I know we can depend on His love. [illegible] Romans 8:28: "And we know that all things work together for good to them that love God [illegible]."

[illegible] the announcement, I spoke. "Tuck, I'd like to go [illegible]."

[illegible]

"[illegible] the first thing tomorrow."

[illegible] Tuck [illegible] his knees beside the bed. [illegible] our Lord, both [illegible] that God heard us, and that He was [illegible] of the whole situation.

If God is in command of your circumstances, what do you [illegible]? [illegible] and that's what we did, [illegible] quiet and [illegible]. We had enjoyed a [illegible] evening and looked forward to the New Year [illegible] that Jesus is Lord over every [illegible].

At Tuck's [illegible] to turn off the light [illegible] into the darkness. "[illegible] it will be [illegible]," [illegible] he held me tight until [illegible].

2
Temporary Pleasures or Lasting Joy?

It was quiet in the motel room when I awoke. By turning my head slightly, I could see Tuck's outline underneath the covers. Dawn would soon flood the room with light. Sleep had not come easily this night.

I patted my husband's shoulder, gently. *Mustn't awaken him. We have a long drive back home to Raleigh today. . . . How I love this man, Lord! Thank God he is with me, especially now.*

As I lay in the semi-darkness, I began the New Year by thanking God for my husband and for the way He had led us through all the years of our marriage. Many of those years had not been easy, but our love for each other was always stronger than our difficulties. I had a feeling I'd be leaning even more heavily upon that love in the days ahead. From somewhere deep within, a sigh escaped my lips as I thought about the possible consequences of the lump I had found yesterday. As my imagination began trying to paint all sorts of gloomy scenarios, I forced my thoughts to turn from the future back to the time before I met Tuck, and before I made Jesus the Lord of my life—all the way back to my little-girl-hood. Although I found some painful memories there, I refused to allow my mind to dwell on them. I knew the Lord was in the process of healing the past. Besides, it's always better to remember the happy times.

As I ran the reels of my mind backward into time, searching for happy thoughts to focus upon, the pain of the present flickered across the screen of my memory. *Must joy always be etched with bitter sweets?* I remembered from my childhood that the thrill of getting something I wanted very badly never lasted long, and that the desire for something else never left me. It seemed that this principle was forever operating in my life.

I remembered the time when my beloved Aunt Helen Polston, for whom I was named, brought me an antique music box from France. It was made of lovely pale-blue wood, inlaid with mother-of-pearl. Had I known what the word *exquisite* meant, I probably would have called it that. Delighted with its lilting little tune and fragile beauty, I played it night and day, hours without end, winding and rewinding its sturdy little stem until it wouldn't budge another inch. One moonlit night, the desire to hear my little box was so strong that I crept out of bed. Afraid to go downstairs alone in the dark, I tugged my sleepy-eyed sister Millie along with me, urging her to listen to the tinkling melody as I played it over and over.

As the days passed, however, the music box was forgotten for longer and longer periods as other interests took its place—learning to play a harmonica, then the Jew's harp. None of these pleasures satisfied me for very long. Always there was a wistful tug at the heart as I realized that again I had lost that fleeting feeling of happiness.

Was it because I was a "handicapped child" that nothing brought me permanent satisfaction? As that question arose in my mind, some of the *painful* memories of my childhood came right behind it. I had been only eighteen months old when I became ill with osteomyelitis, and the memory of that illness lay below the surface of my conscious mind. I could vaguely recall the prolonged series of hospitalizations and painful operations that followed, lasting until I was almost four. As a result of this disease, my right leg was shorter than my left. The rejection I experienced as a weak little girl who couldn't keep up with the other children had left emotional scars more deforming than those on my leg. The more I competed with other children, the more frantic I became to succeed.

My hour of triumph finally came when I reached adolescence and—miracle of miracles!—the boys began to pay me some attention. *Crippled or not,* I thought defiantly, *I have plenty of boyfriends*! Although I wasn't allowed to date until I was sixteen, I learned to flirt much earlier than that—sometimes with two or three boys during the same period. What a fascinating game! Innocent, unaware of pitfalls, I enjoyed each flirtation until, inevitably, the thrill faded, to be replaced by dissatisfaction. I was always surprised and disappointed when this happened. *Why did nothing last*?

By the time I was fifteen, racing horses and entering them in rodeos provided longer-lasting pleasure than anything else I had found. Learning to ride horses seemed to come easily to me, and this skill helped to compensate for the feelings of inferiority created by my physical handicap. I soon graduated from Western saddles to English saddles, and finally learned to ride bareback. I never rode in competition, but Daddy usually took me and my sisters to the rodeos to watch our entries. It was all so exciting!

As soon as I received my driver's license, it became a daily after-school ritual to drive Daddy's little green coupe (complete with rumble seat) down to Uncle Jimmie Polston's riding stable. I watched "my" thoroughbreds both inside and outside the ring, feasting my eyes on their beauty. The horses really belonged to Uncle Jimmie, but he allowed me to name them, and I pretended they were mine.

Down at the stables, I soon made another discovery: *cowboys*! What an exciting life they led! I sat on the rail fence day after day and watched those sun-tanned, blue-jeaned heroes as they worked with Uncle Jimmie's "half-broke" horses. Blue eyes wide with wonder, I admired the cowboys as they strutted out of the back gate and walked bravely up to the nervous beasts. Grabbing the rope halter in one hand, the cowboy jumped onto the frightened animal's back. After that, it was cowboy against horse. Nostrils flared, sweat flowing from trembling flanks, the horse would rear, buck, and plunge around the corral, trying to rid himself of the unaccustomed weight of the rider on his back. Sometimes he threw the cowboy against the fence—but miraculously, the rider was seldom hurt, and I soon learned to jump out of the way.

Soon all the cowboys knew me and took time to talk to me teasingly. Before long, they were teaching me the tricks of their trade—and eventually Daddy gave me a half-tamed black stallion of my own. Since he had a white half-star on his forehead, I named him "Star." For a time, Star was the most important thing in my life.

Then one day—quite unexpectedly—something happened that made horses seem almost unimportant. I fell in love!

The cowboy who suddenly became the light of my life was named Earl, and he had come all the way from Nevada to work for Uncle Jimmie. He wore his black, wide-brimmed cowboy hat cocked on one side of his bright blond hair in a way that almost threw me into a case of the vapors. (I had read that word in *Little Women* when I was a child, and it sounded important.) Now my longing had *two* objects. I still loved the horses with all my heart, except for the secret part I saved for Earl.

I knew he didn't care for me as I did for him, but love ignored this reality. My days were spent thinking of some way to express my devotion to my beloved. The long-sought opportunity to be alone with him finally arrived. Auntie Helen, a wise and wonderful woman, suggested to Earl that he take me to the store to buy some eggs so that she could make an angel food cake.

Overjoyed at the prospect of being alone with my cowboy, I climbed into Uncle Jimmie's beautiful blue touring car beside him. As the Ford chugged down the rambling lane and entered the highway traffic, I chattered nervously to drown out the hammering of my heart. Earl laughed and joked and sang real loud, then suddenly began to whistle. I thought I would faint with ecstasy. No mockingbird's song ever sounded so beautiful as Earl's whistling. *This must be heaven,* I thought.

All too soon, the little country store was there in front of us, squatting in the shade like a tired old man. Earl opened the door for me, and I pulled my pleated skirt tight around my knees before stepping out onto the running board and then to the ground. Together, we walked through the bright sunlight into the store. As I danced through the door beside my tall, gallant cowboy, everyone inside turned to look at us. I felt that the whole world was mine!

After Earl bought the eggs, we climbed back into the car and headed toward the country lane. I'd have to make my move soon if I was ever going to make one. What would it be? Should I reach over and touch his hand, or should I just come out and tell him I loved him? *Oh, I'll just die! What to do? No more time to plan.*

There was the familiar row of crape myrtles. Soon we'd be back at Uncle Jimmie's, and my opportunity would be lost forever. I opened my mouth to speak. Horror of horrors, only a wee little croak came out. *Was that my voice?*

Suddenly, it was too late. Earl had stopped the car, and I hadn't done one thing, said one word. Struggling to get the lump out of my throat, I moved slowly toward the open car door as Earl stood waiting for me to climb out. I thought I'd just die from the love of him. He flashed a smile at me and then—I couldn't believe it—he touched my hand. The whole world swam. I sat there transfixed, until I finally noticed that he was trying to hand me the egg carton. "Will you please take these to Mrs. Polston?" he asked politely. "I've got to check the horses at the barn."

Through the fog of love that enveloped me, I reached out my hand for the eggs. The next moment—I'll never know just how it happened—I felt the awful crunch of cardboard in my trembling fingers. Looking down through bewildered, love-dimmed eyes, I saw a ghastly sight: my handsome cowboy standing beside the car, his beautiful black shirt covered with slimy yellow egg yolks.

I don't remember much about what happened next, but I can recall sobbing in Aunt Helen's bedroom, and her quiet assurance that we didn't need a cake anyway.

The next time I saw Earl, he was sitting astride a glistening, five-gaited Tennessee walker. With some puzzlement, I noted that I was more taken with this new horse than I was with the cowboy. *Will real love never happen to me*? I wondered. *After all, I'm already sixteen*!

3

What Is the Matter with Me?

The new day announced its arrival by slinging bolts of vivid color across the eastern horizon. Looking out our window, I watched the rays of the rising sun begin to streak the sky above the dark-blue waters. Once again, God was making up earth's face.

I sighed and turned to look at Tuck, sleeping so quietly beside me. He hadn't even stirred during my flirtation with the cowboy from my past. How thankful I was that neither Earl nor the fraternity man to whom I was briefly engaged had become a permanent part of my life!

I glanced around the motel room. Nothing seemed to have changed since our arrival the day before, yet everything was different. I wondered how the sun could come up, appear so normal on this morning of my soul's deepest anguish. Last night, it was easy to be confident of God's deliverance. But on this first morning of the new year, the dangers I was facing seemed more real than my faith.

Don't allow yourself to think negatively, I commanded myself. *Satan would love to defeat you through your thought patterns.* My mind raced up and down, searching for something light and pleasant to think about. Again, I forced myself to think backward instead of looking to the threatening uncertainties of the year ahead.

Actually, I had been "in love" almost every new semester during my days in junior college. Each time, I thought it was the real thing, but only once did I accept an engagement ring. My fiancé was an aeronautics major—tall, vivacious, and blond, reminding me of a young palomino. We played tennis every afternoon and went dancing every weekend I could get off the college campus. I felt sure there had never been a girl as happy as I.

Then my beloved graduated from college and announced his plans to join the Air Force. I had never wanted to marry a pilot. If he wanted to *fly* planes, why did he learn to *design* them? Brokenhearted, I reluctantly kissed him good-bye for the first of many times. There followed months of tears and scenes, trains and planes; then finally it was all over. I returned his fraternity pin and engagement ring and made a vow never to trust any other man as long as I lived. At the ripe old age of nineteen, I became a confirmed skeptic where men were concerned.

Three months later, my father announced that our family would be leaving our home in Mullins, South Carolina, and moving to Whiteville, North Carolina. What did I care? My heart would be no less broken in one state than in another. After numerous good-bye parties, sprinkled with tears, warm embraces, and promises to "keep in touch," Mom and Dad, my three sisters, and I closed the door on the home in which we four girls had done most of our growing up.

A few days later, our loaded car turned into the driveway of our new home in Whiteville. A faint stirring of curiosity about what lay ahead in this new town quickened my pulse ever so slightly. The arrival of the moving van the next afternoon, followed by the challenge of settling into a new house, provided a little more excitement. By the time the novelty of different surroundings started to fade, I was beginning to think that perhaps I just *might* like this new town. The lovely old two-story house seemed interesting, and I *did* have a bedroom of my own for the first time in my life.

Three days after we moved in, the telephone had not yet been installed. "Helen, drive down to the telephone office," my dad suggested, "and see if they have forgotten our request. You'll see the building on Pinckney Street beyond the courthouse square." Since our new home was on Pinckney, I felt confident of finding the way.

As I headed Dad's car toward town, I could see the majestic old courthouse directly in front of me, presiding over the square like a setting hen guarding her biddies. Guiding the light-green Studebaker carefully around the square, I drove slowly through town, reading the name of each street as I passed the marker: *Jefferson, Washington, Lee*. I never dreamed that many of these streets had been laid out and named by a young surveyor-lawyer who was to become my father-in-law.

Along Pinckney Street, beautiful old homes sat well back from the sidewalk, surrounded by freshly mowed lawns, hedges of green shrubbery, and lush flower gardens. Camellia and azalea bushes were everywhere. Magnolia trees, crape myrtles, and deep-green boxwoods lined the sidewalks. Whiteville was a beautiful town. *I just might enjoy living here,* I thought. In spite of my determination to be a martyr, suffering the loss of love with obvious and admirable courage, I felt a gentle flush of hope rising within my broken heart.

Finding the phone company's office was no trouble at all, and it was an easy matter to fill out the forms necessary to expedite the installation of our telephone. Mission accomplished, I headed back toward the courthouse square and home. Parking the car in front of the house, I hummed a tune as I bounced up the cement walk in my new plaid blazer, accordion-pleated skirt, and saddle oxfords. I didn't know why I was feeling happier now. For no reason at all—or perhaps because of the family celebration planned for my twentieth birthday tomorrow—I felt, for the moment, content.

A few minutes later, one of our next-door neighbors came walking over. "Mrs. Polston," she said to Mother, "the nice young lawyer who lives across the street just saw your daughter going up your walk and wants to meet her." I thought, *Who cares?* How could a mere stranger understand that I had made a lifelong commitment never to get involved with another man, no matter what? Men were always so disappointing! Politely, but with a defensive sense of superiority, I declined to meet this "nice young lawyer," neighbor or not. The moment was soon forgotten.

"Everybody listen! We now have a phone," I announced to the family when the phone rang the next day. Picking up the receiver with a wide sweep of my arm, I dramatically intoned a "Hel-*LO*!"

"May I speak to Helen?" a pleasant male voice asked.

"This is Helen," I replied with some surprise. Who could be calling so soon after our move?

"Well, I'm Irvin Tucker, your neighbor across the street."

"Oh?" I said rather coolly, surprised at his persistence. Nothing daunted, he asked me for a date, which I refused. How in the world could I enjoy dating a man so much older than I? I could tell from the way he talked that he wasn't like the college boys I was accustomed to dating.

Fortunately for me, Irvin was not easily discouraged. After he had called me three more times in as many days, I realized I was falling in love with a man I knew only as a voice over the telephone. On our first date I found that his "mature sophistication" (he was not quite nine years older than I) only added to his charm. After dating almost every night for three months we became engaged, and two months later we were married. At last, I thought, I had found true happiness!

I felt sure that marriage would be the answer to all my yearnings and unexplained sighing in the night—but it wasn't. Although I truly was in love, I soon realized that romantic love wasn't enough to satisfy me. After two years of continued restlessness, I came to the conclusion that a baby was what I needed to fill the void in my life. Perhaps mother love was the missing ingredient. Soon the son of our love was born—blond, beautiful, bubbly, and all ours! We named him Irvin, III—and to avoid confusion, I began calling my husband by his nickname, "Tuck."

Years passed, bringing traumas and joys, heartaches and pleasures—all wrapped up in patches of time and tied together by love. Still, my heart remained restless. *Our son needs a companion,* I decided. Seven years after the birth of our first child, his brother Laurence arrived.

Repeat of joys and sorrows, fun and frustration. *Restless heart, why do you yearn? You have it all: a devoted husband with a successful law practice, two precious children, a respected place in the community, and a whole fistful of up-to-date charge accounts. Why are you filled with discontent?*

"Would you like a new car, honey?" Tuck inquired. "A house?"

"Yes! A house of our own. This apartment is too small for our family, and we really do need to trade cars."

So Tuck's parents gave us a small cottage they owned, and we bought a shiny new automobile. Later, my dad presented us with a membership in the country club. None of these coveted possessions brought me satisfaction for more than a few days.

"Are you tired of the country club?" my patient husband asked me. "We'll take another weekend trip to Myrtle Beach. . . . Oh, are you tired of the beach? Let's rent a house in the mountains for a few days. It might be a nice change."

"No!"

O God, what is contentment? I did not understand my own discontent. I had never heard St. Augustine's words, "Thou hast made us for Thine own, and our hearts are restless until they find their rest in Thee." If I *had* heard them, they would have meant nothing to me at that time.

One particular day is etched in my memory. The afternoon was blue-skyed, sunshiny, with fleecy clouds. It was springtime, Sunday in the sweet South—my favorite time and place in the whole world. Our family was setting out for a drive to Lake Waccamaw to have dinner at The Anchorage—a pleasant gathering spot for local people.

Glancing down at our two-year-old holding hands with his nine-year-old brother as we walked to the shiny new car, I thought, *Our little family would make a typical picture for the cover of some health magazine, or perhaps a Sunday-school periodical—all dressed up and sunshiny all over.* I had a penchant for dressing the boys in Eton suits: short pants, wide white collars and Eton caps, plus knee socks and sandals, all ordered from Best's in New York. We may have been "small town," but we knew about big-city ways.

The sigh inside me threatened to erupt into a sob. I hoped Tuck hadn't heard. *I am so unhappy,* I thought. *What Is the Matter with Me?*

4

The Answer

As if he *had* heard that stifled sob in my memories, Tuck moaned softly. I hoped he was getting ready to wake up and face this new year with me—but his regular breathing soon let me know he had returned to a deep sleep. For a while longer, I was alone to struggle with my rising panic. Again I forced my thoughts away from the present. . . . *What can I think about now?* My brief career as a writer—*that* was an interesting memory!

It began when our boys were eleven and four. As day followed day, with no diminution in my restlessness, the thought came to me, *I love to write . . . think I'll send some poems to the state-capital paper.* They were soon published: one, another, then several others. *How about the local paper? Free-lance—that's what I'll do.*

I went to see the editor of our paper—himself a Pulitzer-prize winner. Editor liked the articles I took him and wanted more. Soon I was writing a weekly column. Then the mayor wanted me to write some articles for him, and I did. The Columbus County Library asked me to write book reviews, and I did that too.

One day, I happened to hear a national radio show featuring stories about ordinary people in the United States. On an impulse, I wrote up my experiences as a Cub Scout leader and submitted the manuscript to the address given. A few weeks later, a call came from the producers of the program. Would I come to New York and share my story with their listeners? And would I bring my whole family with me and spend several days in the city as the guest of the network? They especially wanted to meet our son Irvin, the Cub Scout who was responsible for my interest in scouting.

Would I? Surely such an experience would supply me with enough excitement to transform my life forever!

During the broadcast, I was presented with a beautiful jeweled key to the city. They told me it would open any door in New York, "from the mayor's office on down. Just ask for whatever you want," they said, "and if it's possible, we'll get it for you."

They lived up to their promise: doors opened wherever we wanted to enter. We were given fabulous hotel accommodations, meals in gourmet restaurants, a tour of the city, a drive through Central Park in a hansom cab, a boat trip around Manhattan Island, tickets to anything we desired to attend, and—best and most necessary of all—a chauffeur-driven limousine to take us where we were supposed to be at the time we were supposed to be there.

We spent a week in New York, being treated like royalty, wondering all the time why and *if* this was really happening to us. On the day of our departure, I took advantage of a moment alone with the famous host of the radio show to ask how I had been singled out for such attention. Taking me into the mailroom, he showed me hundreds of mailbags stacked against the wall. "That's just *this* week's mail," he told me. "We chose your story, out of the thousands of submissions received that week, because it was unique."

"Unique?" I asked. "In what way?"

"Well," he replied, "you're the only one who ever challenged us to prove that the Statue of Liberty really has a heart. We decided to prove to our radio audience through your family that the Lady in the Harbor has a heart as big as the whole of New York City."

On the flight home, Tuck and I shared a laugh over this disclosure. So all the pomp and circumstance really had nothing to do with us or our achievements. The network simply wanted to polish its image and prove a point—and we were the beneficiaries.

New York City was wonderful to our family, but nothing touched our hearts so much as the welcome we received from our hometown folks when we returned to Whiteville. Surely, my life from that time on would be filled with new meaning and fresh purpose. I didn't really know *how* this would be accomplished, but I felt a fresh spark of hope.

After only a few days, however, I began to taste again the familiar flavor of boredom. Determined to find some other source of excitement, I set up my secondhand portable typewriter on the dining-room table. Our family could eat all our meals in the kitchen while I fulfilled my destiny as a world-renowned author.

Putting the children in the care of The Maid, I dared anyone to come near me while I was writing. For a brief period, the urge to compose took precedence even over my family's interests.

Such was the case one morning when I was in a deep fog of creativity and eleven-year-old Irvin dashed into the hallowed writing room. He was screaming at the top of his youthful lungs: "Mother, there's a snake on my rope swing! Come kill 'im!"

"Get out of here," I yelled in return, "or there's going to be something worse than that on the seat of your pants!" As I reached toward the familiar green switch that was kept handy for just such interruptions, the look of hurt on Irvin's face touched a sensitive place in my heart. Nevertheless, I suppressed my maternal instinct and shook the switch in his direction, taking satisfaction in my son's hasty exit from the room.

Just then, The Maid stuck her head through the door and shouted toward the typewriter, "Miss Helen, there's a snake near-bout big as my arm out there under the boys' swing!" Writing forgotten, I made a mad dash to the backyard. I got there just in time to see The Yard Man dispose of the reptile with a final slash of his hoe. Leaning over, he lifted up a huge copperhead, still wiggling, for my guilt-filled eyes to behold.

As I looked at the awed faces of my sons and the neighborhood children who had gathered to watch, the creative fire in me was effectively extinguished. I was appalled by the realization of what my self-centered desire for "fulfillment" had almost cost my precious family. After seeing to the snake's proper burial, I walked inside the house, closed my typewriter, and put it in the storeroom. For the present, at least, my writing career was ended.

Once again, I tried to find fulfillment in my home and family, in friends and social gatherings and bridge clubs, in civic work and church work. Still the emptiness remained in my heart.

At about this time, Tuck accepted an appointment as a federal chief assistant district attorney. For several months, he spent his weeks in Raleigh, North Carolina, and his weekends in Whiteville. His prolonged absences made my life seem even more devoid of meaning.

I sought counsel from my minister, who suggested that I might find answers if I got involved in teaching a Sunday-school class. I took this assignment for a while, without noticeable benefit either to me or to the class of "young marrieds." Then, at the pastor's request, I served for a spell as "front-door greeter" for the Sunday-morning worship services. I shook hands with many lovely people, but none of them supplied the answer I was seeking. In a sermon one morning, the minister read one of my poems, entitled "Who Am I?"—but it failed to bring about even a modest revival. Not a curious response from a soul in the congregation. I was still no closer to finding out who I was, or what was wrong with me.

Tuck and I both knew, however, that it was wrong for us to be separated. We decided it was time to move our family to Raleigh, so that we could be together again. The boys needed their father, and Tuck and I needed each other.

I dreaded the thought of leaving our Whiteville friends and starting all over in a strange town. With so few inner resources, how could I face such a major adjustment? I *had* to find a solution for my restlessness and lack of inner peace.

In desperation, I finally went to see Bea—one of my best friends, my bridesmaid, the longtime, loyal, double-dating companion of my youth. "Bea, can you tell this weary, disillusioned, thirty-year-old woman what it takes to find peace?"

Through my fog of despair, I wondered why Bea didn't appear to be surprised at my question. For a long time she continued to sit at her dressing table, making up her lovely face. Turning to me at last, she replied, "I don't know, but I know someone who can tell us."

Did Bea say "us"? Does that mean she's dissatisfied with her life too?

Bea's voice filtered through my thoughts: "Her name is Sarah."

"Who is this wonder woman, Sarah?"

"You'll see," Bea answered with a knowing smile.

The next day—a rainy, foggy morning in October, 1953—Bea and I waited in her living room for her "woman of peace." Sarah appeared at the door right on time—a small woman with beautiful blond hair swept off a radiant face. After introductions, Bea said, "Sarah, can you tell Helen how to be happy?"

Bea didn't have to put it that *bluntly,* I thought. But by now I was so desperate I didn't really care. I glanced at Sarah. Such a smile! How could anyone be so obviously content? Drawing a little footstool near my chair, Sarah sat serenely looking up into my face. Her joy began to penetrate the layers of unsatisfied longing that were smothering my spirit. As she began to tell about Jesus, I felt unfamiliar emotion stirring deep within me. I wished Sarah wouldn't look at me so intently, though. It made me uncomfortable. I glanced over at Bea, hoping she would somehow come to my rescue—but her attention was totally focused on what Sarah was saying.

Suddenly, I did the unthinkable: I lost control and began to weep all over Bea's *Mademoiselle* magazine, which I was holding as a security blanket. Sarah waited. "Never mind," I was finally able to say. "I'll be all right"—but I knew I *wouldn't* be, without help.

"Helen, if you really want peace of mind, you must ask the Prince of Peace to give it to you," Sarah said. "If you invite Jesus to come into your heart, He will satisfy your longing and give you true happiness." Seeing that I was unable to reply, she continued gently, "Do you want to ask Him to forgive your sins? Everyone has sinned, you know."

"Don't go any further," I interrupted, between sobs. "I do, I do! But first I want to go home and be alone for a while." Sarah nodded understandingly, then quickly scribbled something on a piece of paper and handed it to me.

Still weeping, I left Bea's house unceremoniously and headed my little blue coupe toward home. I parked the car in the driveway and hurried into the house, slamming the door behind me. In the familiar blue-and-white living room, I ran over to the sofa and dropped to my knees. Searching for the words Sarah had used, I began haltingly to ask Jesus to forgive my sins and come into my heart. Soon the words of confession and petition began to flow naturally from my lips and I *knew* He was listening to me.

I didn't see anything with my eyes or hear anything with my ears; but as joy flooded my being, I knew I had found what my restless heart had been seeking all my life. *It was Jesus,* the Son of God! Since childhood, I had acknowledged Him with my lips and known about Him with my mind, but now my heart knew Him too. "He is real!" I said aloud.

Just at that moment, a gentle gust of wind blew the front door ajar. As I rose from my knees to shut it, an indescribable peace fell upon me, enveloping me in Love. Although I didn't know it then, I had been born again (see John 3:3); I had become a "new creature" in Christ Jesus (see 2 Corinthians 5:17).

Lost in the wonder of this miracle that had happened to me, I forgot about the scrap of paper Sarah had given me. When I found it later that afternoon, I discovered that she had jotted down references to several passages of Scripture:

Romans 3:23; 5:8; 10:9	Acts 2:38,39; 16:31
John 3:16,17,36; 6:37	2 Corinthians 5:17
Ephesians 2:8–10	1 Timothy 2:5,6
1 John 5:11–13	Luke 13:3

That night I stayed up long after Tuck had gone to bed, searching out the verses written on that piece of paper, then reading and rereading them. For the first time in my life the Bible made sense to me, and I wanted to devour its pages. The Son of God was telling me all about Himself, and about life and people and how to handle problems and my personal everyday situations. I couldn't get enough of it!

The next morning, I could hardly wait to visit Bea and tell her what had happened to me after I left her house in tears the day before. At last—at *last*—I told her, I had found the key to fulfillment and to the true joy that no one and no *thing* could take from me (see John 16:22). Bea eagerly drank in all I had to say—and before I had finished sharing, she gave *her* life to Jesus.

So many years ago, I thought, *and how faithfully she still walks with Him*! That happy thought reminded me of the young-married class the minister had encouraged me to teach. God must have been in that appointment after all. Within a month after Bea and I were born again, four members of my Sunday-school class experienced the new birth for themselves. What a Savior! If He could do all that, He could certainly heal my body too.

Tuck stirred beside me, as my thoughts returned to the present. This lump in my breast must be dealt with—but how? Questions raced through my mind, bringing perplexity and momentary panic.

"Lord," I whispered into the now-sunlit motel room, "You promised to be with me always. [See Matthew 28:20.] You said You'd never leave me or forsake me." [See Hebrews 13:5.] Remembrance of the promises brought comfort. Once again, blessed assurance had come.

After a simple breakfast, Tuck and I took a short walk on the beach before packing for our trip home. The bright sunshine, golden sand, and shimmering, deep-blue water seemed to surround us with glory. Tuck took my hand in his and we stepped up our pace, breathing deeply of the fresh, stimulating sea air as we walked. I glanced back at our tracks in the sand.

Lord, I prayed silently, *I love life. Please, can't I live to complete my time?*

As if in answer to my prayer, another promise from His Word came to my mind: "I will take sickness away from the midst of thee. . . . The number of thy days I will fulfil" (Exodus 23:25,26).

I gave Tuck's hand a squeeze. "Come on," I said, suddenly filled with vigor and hope. "Let's see if we can get home in time for the bowl games."

5

Entrance to a Strange Land

On the trip back to Raleigh, Tuck and I had begun praying that the Lord would direct us to the surgeon of His choice. As soon as we entered the office of the doctor to whom my gynecologist had referred me, I felt sure this prayer had been answered.

One of my personal foibles is that of giving people private nicknames to match their outstanding characteristics. I caught a brief glimpse of my new doctor walking down a hall, and the name "Strong-Flower" popped into my mind. It was a name that proved to be symbolic of his strength and gentleness, synonymous with his real name. I liked it.

Nurse True-Calling was standing behind the reception desk. Greeting us with a cheerful smile, she gave the impression of being totally in command of the situation. In an effort to put us at ease, she explained that, in a few minutes, she would take me into the examining room, where the doctor would see me. Then we could "go on from there."

I didn't know where "there" was, but I was impressed with Nurse True-Calling and with her genuine concern for me as a person. Eventually, Tuck and I learned that the entire office staff was characterized by the professional dedication we recognized in Nurse

True-Calling—a dedication that reflected Dr. Strong-Flower's commitment to meeting *all* the needs of his patients, emotional as well as physical.

After a short wait, Nurse True-Calling came to escort me into the tiny examining room. There she handed me an interesting little gown, a half-affair that barely covered the home front and left nothing else to the imagination. As I undressed, she gave me the reassuring information that hundreds of thousands of women go through this examination every year and that approximately 75 percent "come out all right"—that is, they don't have cancer.

"But how about the 38,000 women in the United States who die of breast cancer every year—and the 119,000 who will discover this year that they have it?" I asked warily, looking hopefully across the table at her even though I wasn't comfortable with the grim statistics that had greeted me from the front page of the newspaper.

"Now, Mrs. Tucker," she chided, "you're crossing the bridge before you get to it. Let's go back to the 75 percent who *don't* have it when they think they might. Think positively."

When she saw that didn't quite satisfy, that I was still holding onto my, "But what if—" stance, she tried another tack, with a smile.

"Even if you do have a malignancy, more effective treatments are being discovered all the time that reduce the mortality rate. Cancer isn't the bugaboo fatal disease it once was. Besides, you haven't even been examined yet. Let's just wait and see—"

Nurse True-Calling had hardly gotten me on the examining table and covered my embarrassed flesh with a flimsy paper sheet when Dr. Strong-Flower entered the room. As soon as I heard his warm greeting, I realized I had a friend. I was aware of personal strength and integrity when I looked into his eyes. Kindness radiated from him, and his manner reflected the gentleness of God. I knew in my heart that this man was God's choice for my surgeon.

After asking me a few questions, Dr. Strong-Flower asked me to locate the lump for him. As his sensitive fingers examined my breast, I watched his face for any expression that might betray his thoughts. Somewhat to my surprise, he asked me if I had any idea how large the lump was. When I estimated a measure on my little finger, he smiled at the childish gesture.

"I think you're right," he said, "and you do have a lump." Then, in the warm professional manner that characterized him, he told me to get dressed and come into his office.

As he left the room, he sent Nurse True-Calling to summon Tuck to his office. A feeling of uneasiness spurred me on to dress in record time. *Why must I wait for his diagnosis? Why couldn't he say something*—anything—*to give me a hint? Does he think I have cancer? What does he know?*

I felt teary-eyed as the three of us sat in Dr. Strong-Flower's office, discussing my case. In an effort to distract myself, I carefully studied the pictures on his walls; but my pretended interest in the doctor's family portraits was soon dispelled by words like "surgery" and "chances are good." Slowly, the reality dawned on me that Dr. Strong-Flower was not talking about drawing fluid from a cyst that would "just go away." He was setting a date for an *operation,* and I was the patient. I would need to go in for a biopsy, he explained. If that showed malignant cells, further surgery would be needed.

After saying, "I hope to get a room very soon," Dr. Strong-Flower suggested to my husband that a private room might be advisable. Something in the tone of his voice recalled *For Whom the Bell Tolls,* and I asked him if I would have a long stay in the hospital.

"Not necessarily," he replied; "but *if* it takes more than a few days, we want your stay to be as pleasant as possible."

Just then, Nurse True-Calling came into the office with a big smile on her face. "You must be living right," she said to me. "You'll have a room in just eight days."

Eight days? Eight days to think! Eight days to worry! *What will I do with all those hours, Lord? . . . Lord, are You sure about this?*

He was sure. And He used those eight days to do what He does better than any psychiatrist: listen to me. I spent the better part of that waiting period on the floor of our family room—fasting much of the time, praying, reading my Bible, and being turned upside down and inside out.

I had confessed my sins many times before, but now I did it again. Before I entered that hospital, I wanted to be *positive* that no unconfessed sin stood between me and the Lord. I wasn't motivated by a fear of death, for I did not expect to die. I had long wanted all of my life to be pure and holy and clean, but now I wanted it with renewed urgency.

One very special day, I closed my eyes and thought over my life. I acknowledged that I am a self-indulgent, careless, sometimes indifferent person; sometimes too casual, often caring too much;

loyal to a fault, spontaneous, temperamental, talkative, rarely silent, wounded easily when I should be self-forgetting, passive when I should be active, and active when passivity would be appropriate.

"Lord, I'm full of so many wordy remarks when silence would better heal. How can You ever do anything with such a life? No wonder I stay in hot water—when I should be trusting and at peace."

Tears of desperation dropped into the golden carpet. "I'm a helpless, hopeless mess, and if You don't clean me up, I am sunk, Lord."

I continued confessing my sins as they came to mind. I knew the Savior was listening, forgiving, and cleansing me. I also knew that Jesus was preparing me for whatever was to come. He's my trustworthy friend, my very own Mediator. I counted on Him to plead my case before the Father. His Word says He will (see I Timothy 2:5 and Hebrews 7:24–26), and I had a feeling I'd be needing His help badly in the days to come.

I lay silent for a long time, until gradually I became conscious of feeling chilled. Then I noticed that my forehead was wet with perspiration. Is it possible to be afraid and not recognize the symptoms? To have outward calm masking inward fear? Could this "great and faithful Christian" also be experiencing panic? What a witness! *I am petrified*!

I leaned heavily against the green-and-gold sofa in our family room, feeling the softness of velvet under my arms. It seemed like an old friend. Sitting on the floor with my head against it brought momentary comfort—something I sorely needed.

Why am I so afraid? I have His promises, and they should be enough. For years I've believed and taught, "God's Word is true!" Will it fail me now? . . . Never! I'm *the one that's failing. Lord, HELP ME!*

In my family, cancer is an all-too-familiar disease: three cases in three generations. Would I be number four? *Lord, my heart is failing me for fear*! *Will I fail You too? I don't mind dying, Jesus, but I can't bear the thought of dying by inches.*

I felt hot—no, cold. *Where will I go? What should I do? Is this panic? It must be. There's no hope, Lord*!

As the questions and anxious forebodings gained momentum in my mind, I felt a momentary desire to break and run. I thought of Star, the little half-tamed stallion I had when I was a teenager. He'd bare his teeth at me, then break gait and dash helter-skelter. I wanted to do the same thing now—but what would the neighbors think?

Feeling as though my eyes were bulging out of my head, I ran my fingers through my hair, seeking relief. How numb my scalp felt under the pressure! Was I losing my mind? *Think of some Scripture; it never fails. Lord, help! Give me a verse!*

Immediately there came to my mind, "For God hath not given us the spirit of fear; but of power, and of love, and of a sound mind" (2 Timothy 1:7). *If He hasn't given me this spirit of fear, then I refuse it. That's what to do: refuse it!*

Remembering the instructions given in God's Word for handling this situation, I said aloud, "Satan, in the name of Jesus Christ I refuse the spirit of fear. It is written, 'Submit yourselves therefore to God. Resist the devil, and he will flee from you' [James 4:7]. So be gone, in the name of Jesus!"

What a price I had paid for my panic, my fear! They were blocking all the help God wanted to give me. Again speaking out loud, I said to the devil, "I'm a child of God! He said He would never leave me or forsake me. [See Hebrews 13:5.] I will not let you entangle me in a bondage of fear."

My mind began to grow calm, and my racing heart responded by slowing its rhythm. For a long time I lay on the carpet, looking up at the ceiling. Scripture after Scripture floated into my mind. I quoted them aloud, claiming them one by one to the Father. I have no idea how long I lay there, but I know that hours passed and the tears flowed freely. Telephone and door bells rang; I didn't move to answer them. It was a crucial time. Talking aloud to Jesus, I gave honest verbal expression to my feelings in this crisis I was undergoing.

I remembered the year 1961, when my dad was dying with lung cancer. His little white Bible, the binding worn and frayed, always lay within easy reach on the windowsill right beside his bed. It was usually open to the Psalms. *Will I be like him? He was so brave and uncomplaining. Lord, let me be brave!*

Near the end of his illness, Daddy asked me if I would "be coming." I knew what he meant: Would I be coming to heaven? When I assured him we all would, he just seemed to let go of his life. In a few days, God released him from his frail body. It was time for him to go Home.

Why did that come to mind? I'm not going to die! Oh, Lord, if only . . . My mind kept wanting to slip its moorings of faith and drift off into the dangerous waters of fear and rebellion. *Jesus, if I can't count on You to see me through this terrible ordeal, then I can't count on You at all.*

By the time Tuck came home from the office at seven, I was enough in control to go through the familiar routine of preparing supper, then eating with him. We didn't share our usual chitchat about the day's activities but were mostly quiet. Finally bedtime came, and with it some sense of relief. I felt sorry for Tuck. I knew it was difficult for him to have to act brave and maintain his self-control.

After showering, I paddled into the bedroom in my old tangerine terry robe to tell Tuck that the bath was all his. After he had begun his shower, I was standing alone by the dressing table when I suddenly felt the overwhelming presence of the Holy Spirit surrounding me. I whirled about, fully expecting to see Jesus. He had appeared to others—why not to me too? Although no bodily form was visible to my eyes, I could sense His presence everywhere, filling the room. . . . Why, at a time like this, would I think of Abraham as he lifted the knife over Isaac?

Trembling, I dropped to my knees, then lay flat on the floor, awed by His closeness and waiting to learn His purpose in coming to me. . . . Minutes passed. I could hear the water running in Tuck's shower. I wondered fleetingly how such a supernatural intervention from God could seem so natural.

After a long period of stillness and waiting, confidence of God's direction suddenly flowed into my heart. I rose to my feet and walked over to the mirror. Looking at myself in the reflection, I prayed, "Lord Jesus, Thy will be done with my life. Please heal my body, soul, and spirit. I want to be made whole, a real reflection of You."

Peace. . . . He flooded my whole body, soul, and spirit with Himself. All fear was gone.

6

Room 321

Would you send your helpless child to the hospital alone? Of course not! Neither does our heavenly Father. But as Tuck and I drove up the winding driveway that led to The Hospital, I momentarily forgot that truth. The bitter winter wind howled around us, swaying the automobile and whipping foreboding gusts of icy spray across the windshield. *The sky is gray with tears,* I thought as Tuck circled around and let me out at the admitting entrance.

While he parked the car, I walked alone up the front steps of the hospital, made my way into a strange waiting room, and found a seat. I should have known Jesus would be there. This time, He came to me in the form of a little volunteer in a pink smock. Welcoming me with a glad smile, she handed me some papers to fill out. While I was working on them, she told me her name was Beth. I had already nicknamed her "Glad-Smile," but I used the name she had given me when I introduced her to Tuck—who, by that time, had brought my suitcase from the car to the waiting room.

"It's going to snow for sure tonight," he said as they exchanged small talk. I knew they were both trying to boost my courage, but it didn't help. I was terrified! Why did fear and courage play games with me? Like chessmen on a board, they battled it out within my heart, robbing me of steadfast peace.

With a voice that matched her smile, Beth invited me to come with her to the lab for the necessary blood work. She directed Tuck to the room where anxious friends and relatives wait.

When we reached the lab, the smell of blood was almost overwhelming—or was it my imagination? *Lord*! I cried, somewhere deep within. As if she had heard me, Glad-Smile began to comfort me with reassuring words.

"You're a Christian, aren't you?" I asked her, interrupting.

She seemed surprised at my question. "Yes, I am," she replied after a momentary pause. "How did you know?"

"I just know."

Tears came into her eyes. "I'm a pastor's wife," she told me, "but my husband went to be with the Lord two years ago." She hesitated for a moment, then added, "It was for a reason."

Immediately there was a bond. The realization that the first person to meet me in the hospital was another member of my family made me know that my Father had not left me for a moment. He never does, though I am often without human companions.

After a sample of blood had been drawn from my arm (I kept my eyes closed all the time), I went back out to Mrs. Glad-Smile. We collected Tuck and my little plaid suitcase; then she rang for the elevator and told us good-bye. When the elevator came, we were on our way to my room—Room 321.

With a series of jerks and creaks, the elevator finally came to an undignified halt, depositing Tuck and me onto the third floor. I remembered that The Hospital was in the process of building a new facility to replace this somewhat antiquated one, and that thought brought me a fleeting sense of gratitude—along with profound regret that the new buildings hadn't been completed in time for my tenure.

When Tuck and I turned left, as directed, we came face to face with the thing I most dreaded: the silver swinging doors leading to the operating suite. My heartbeat quickened, perspiration covered my face, my palms felt damp, my mouth became dry. *O, Lord*!

Tuck and I had no trouble finding Room 321, which was only one door away from *those doors. God is in charge,* I reminded myself as we walked into my "private room" and looked around. I could hardly believe what my eyes were seeing.

The room was no larger than a respectable closet. (Indeed, we learned later that it had once been the filing closet for the temporary office next door.) *No wonder they're building another hospital,* I thought, looking about me in dismay.

The room was dominated by the hospital bed, which took up almost its entire length and half its breadth. Curiously opening the closet door, Tuck was taken aback to find it filled with sinister-looking pipes wrapped in black tape, to which a few coat hangers had been wired; there were no rods or hooks for hanging clothes. Quickly, he shut the door. Next we peeped into the little stall of a bathroom, where a sign proclaimed to the world that the room cost $67.77 per day. *I'd think they'd be ashamed to advertise that fact,* I thought gloomily, peering into the dark hole.

Tuck was so upset that he turned and walked quickly out into the hall. Leaning against the tiny combination desk-dresser, I wrestled with my emotions. Wouldn't it be great if I could just explode, bawl someone out, then walk out into the street and go home?

Lord, I'd like to. It's justified!

He read my thoughts. *Praise Me.* The words were barely audible to my listening heart. *Praise Me, Helen.*

Remembering the verses about offering Him the sacrifice of praise and about His giving us "the garment of praise for the spirit of heaviness" (Isaiah 61:3), I knew that a good God had let me have that command to lift my heavy spirit.

The words came slowly, haltingly: "Lord, I praise You. Lord, I love You . . ."

"The name plate on the door has your name on it, and the room number checks with this card," my husband said, coming back into the room. "This is Room 321."

Looking up into his anxious face, my heart melted with love. I lifted his chin with my hand and kissed his cheek.

"Honey, it's all right. It really is!" I told him. How often I would find myself repeating that phrase, to reassure both of us, during the next few days! "Let's just thank the Lord I got admitted."

"No," he said. "I'm going back down to the office and ask for another room. At least I can *ask*." Noting my expression, he hesitated. "You *do* want me to, don't you?"

"Let's just praise Him," I said in reply.

"All right," he answered quietly. Wrapping our arms tightly around each other, we lifted our voices in praise to God. Somehow it no longer mattered about the room.

We were interrupted by Nurse All-Business, who came in to give us instructions about putting my clothes in the closet. Then she directed me to relax and make myself comfortable. I now know that the best way to unnerve a woman is to order her to relax.

Our next visitor was Nurse Come-On-Let's-Hold-Up-Our-Chin, who shooed Tuck out of the room and wrested my new brown pantsuit from me. "You don't sit around here in your street clothes, young lady," she informed me when I expressed reluctance to put on night clothing at that hour of the afternoon. As she coaxed me into the blue satin pajamas I had brought and ordered me into the high-and-lifted-up hospital bed, she kept reminding me, "This is no motel!"—a fact I wasn't in danger of forgetting.

After she left, Tuck and I had the room to ourselves. We didn't talk much. He just pulled the desk chair up close to the bed and held my hand. What was there to say? I felt unnatural propped up in the tall bed when I wasn't sick—*not until tomorrow anyway,* I thought. It was threatening, foreboding, frightening to be here, even with Tuck beside me.

One of Tuck's law partners had thoughtfully given me a small devotional book to bring to the hospital. After supper, Tuck picked it up and spent part of the evening reading aloud from it. Hearing some of my favorite verses soothed me. My mind would grasp a thought, and I'd hang onto it.

When orders came over the loudspeaker for visitors to leave the floor, Tuck kissed me good-night, promising to see me in the morning. Very shortly after his departure, Dr. Sleep, the anesthesiologist, paid a reassuring visit, which helped prepare me emotionally for tomorrow's ordeal. He had hardly gotten out of the room when Preparatory Personnel came in to prepare me *physically.*

When they had finished their unpleasant chores and left me in peace, I tried to put the implications of those two visits out of my mind while I went through my usual bedtime routine. Then I climbed back into bed, turned out the light, and began the business of talking myself to sleep.

I had been storing Bible verses in the reservoir of my mind for some twenty-four years, and now I was able to call on the Word of God for comfort. How I wished that I had spent *more* time memorizing passages I have studied! I once heard a famous evangelist say that he and his family are memorizing Scriptures as fast as they can, so that when the famine of the Word comes upon the earth (see Amos 8:11) their memory banks will be well supplied.

I was glad to find in *my* memory bank the line from Proverbs 3:24 that says, "When thou liest down, thou shalt not be afraid: yea, thou shalt lie down, and thy sleep shall be sweet." After thanking God for that promise and for the sweet sleep He was going to give me, I pictured myself curled up in Jesus' arms and began singing softly, "Jesus Loves Me."

That's the last thing I remember until I suddenly jerked awake, aware that I was freezing! My toes were so cold that I felt sure they would break off if I jumped off the bed—so I reached for the bell. My call for help was answered by Nurse Glad-Tidings, a young black woman whose laughter was contagious.

"No wonder you're cold," she said, feeling my icy feet. "The window's got a hole in it."

Dashing from the room like an actress in a grade-B movie, she returned a few minutes later with plastic to cover my window, hole and all. Then she piled more blankets on my bed, saving one to wrap around my cold feet. While she was taping the plastic to the window, we laughed together about the sign on the bathroom door proudly proclaiming the cost of my "air-conditioned" room. After Nurse Glad-Tidings left, the warmth of her love lingered inside the room.

Curled up tightly under the covers of the strange white bed, I thought of Tuck. By now he would be home, sprawled in the middle of our mahogany four-poster—taking up all the room, as usual. I smiled into the dark at the thought of this dear husband God had given me. While sleet swished briskly against my windowpane, silence filled the halls outside my room, spilling inside to overwhelm me. Thoughts of those giant silver doors through which they'd soon be wheeling me pressed against my mind, demanding a response of fear. The hard mattress on my bed brought little comfort. Everything seemed unfamiliar in this strange, unyielding land.

I'll check out my constant supply, I thought, feeling a surge of hope. Again I began drawing on my memory bank, gaining comfort from the Scriptures.

"Let not your heart be troubled" (John 14:1).

"Lo, I am with you alway, even unto the end . . ." (Matthew 28:20).

"He giveth his beloved sleep" (Psalm 127:2).

I never knew when the precious promises stopped flowing through my mind. One of His beloved had fallen asleep.

7

The Holding Room

When I awoke the next morning—Wednesday, January 11, 1978—the words of an old hymn were running through my head: "Father, if this cup cannot pass away, let me drink it to the full." As I lay in bed listening to the morning sounds of the hospital and wondering what the day would bring, I remembered the commitment I had once made to my God: "Lord, it doesn't matter about me. Whatever You want for my life, I'm willing." And I was. If I was faced with the fact that I had cancer, I would handle it in the knowledge that God was in control of my life and that He had permitted this trial of my faith and commitment to come to me. If I had to face an operation—not merely a look-see, but removal of my breast—I knew He would be with me.

I had spent eight days going over and around and through my life. I'd had eight hard, wonderful days with Him alone, and I felt "confessed up." "Lord Jesus," I prayed, "You've made me feel as pure and clean as a four-year-old. You know I'm ready for whatever this day brings. When I dropped off to sleep last night, I was in Your arms. I can face those swinging doors."

My operation was scheduled for nine o'clock. Long before that hour, Nurse Cheerful-Face came into my room bringing my breakfast: two fat white pills.

"Now you just take these," she said soothingly, "and they'll help you to relax."

Before I gulped down the pills, I said aloud, "Cowards die many times before their deaths; the valiant never taste of death but once" (*Julius Caesar,* Act 2, Scene 2). Nurse Cheerful-Face looked surprised.

"Don't you like Shakespeare?" I teased.

My effort to hide my panic with levity fooled no one, least of all me. I was grateful for the merciful pills and for the gradual relaxation I began to feel. When The Strong Boys brought in the little wheely cart to take me through those swinging doors, I was barely aware that my husband was standing beside me with a sad face. I wanted to pat him and love him and tell him everything was all right, but I couldn't move.

I had dreaded being wheeled to the operating room—but it was during that short ride that I became acutely aware of Someone walking beside me. His nearby presence was unmistakable; even through the fog of medication He made Himself known to me. He was on my right side, near the wall. I knew the Prince of Peace had come to be with me, for I've never felt such peace. As He walked by my side through the dreaded doors, all apprehension vanished.

They pushed my cart over into an alcove in the "holding room," and I looked around. I could see no one, but I was still fully aware of God's presence. I had asked Him to stay close to me through this ordeal, and I felt His closeness now as never before. *God is so faithful,* I thought drowsily.

From somewhere way down deep within my spirit, I heard the words, "*Now* you trust *Me* for your life and not *yourself.* Soon you will be happy." I knew it was the Comforter. I was relaxed. I had let go, and God was in complete control.

I vaguely remembered the prayers that had been offered in my behalf—first by my family and my faithful Tuesday-Morning Prayer Group, and soon by Christians across the entire city of Raleigh and even in surrounding cities. Some of them seemed to be praying that God would "melt the lump" and that it "just wouldn't be there" when I went in for examination. I knew He *could* supernaturally remove the lump, but somehow—I can't explain how—I knew He wasn't going to. In that mysterious, special way He has of preparing the heart, He had prepared my heart for a hospital visit and surgical procedure. But I didn't expect cancer.

God's ways are not our ways, and He doesn't always melt the lumps in our lives. Sometimes He has a purpose in allowing us to undergo surgery or other severe trials. In my own case, I knew there was much the Lord wanted to show me through this dreaded ordeal. If there had been an easier way, He would have chosen it. Because of the physical and emotional traumas I had suffered in childhood, an iceberg of anxiety and fear and resentment was trapped deep within my spirit, and my loving heavenly Father wasn't going to melt the lump in my breast and leave the iceberg there freezing my spirit forever. I didn't want to think about what the thawing process might entail; but for now it was enough that He was with me, surrounding me with His love and filling me with His peace. I marveled at my own serenity as I lay there, completely relaxed, on the little wheely cart.

After a while, I closed my eyes. I may have dropped off to sleep, but I suddenly became aware that someone *human* had moved close to my right side. When I opened my eyes and turned my head to the right, I found myself six inches from a huge man lying on another stretcher with his eyes closed. He must have weighed well over 250 pounds, and he had a head full of curly black hair. He resembled my conception of a truck-driver—long-haul at that! I was just thinking that I'd hate to meet him in a dark alley when he suddenly opened his eyes and looked squarely at me, eyeball-to-eyeball. I closed my eyes tight; but almost immediately my eyelids flew open like window shades. Spontaneously, I stretched out my hand and touched his arm, feeling the muscle under the short sleeve of his hospital gown.

To my own surprise, I heard myself saying to this stranger, "Would you like me to pray for you?" I knew it wasn't my voice that phrased the question, but the Master's voice speaking to a need.

When the man nodded his reply, I recognized his answer as a cry for help—a sincere plea from the very depths of his soul.

I don't remember the words of the prayer; but my Father understood the need in the heart of that man, and I knew He would help him. Before I was through speaking, my eyes closed. When I opened them later, I discovered that The Truck-Driver and his stretcher were gone. I may never see him again, but I know that the Prince of Peace accompanied him through the second set of swinging doors to the operating room. The man had called, and Jesus had answered.

I closed my eyes again, thankful that the presence of the Almighty

One remained with me through the long period of waiting, just as the cloud remained with the Children of Israel in the wilderness.

Surely The Strong Boys would soon be coming to push me down the narrow white hall into the operating theater. Although I knew His presence would go with me through the swinging doors, I needed a further word of reassurance from Him now. Jesus promised His sheep that they would know their Shepherd's voice (see John 10:4), and I had walked with Him long enough to know the truth of that promise. Relying on it in this time of need, I whispered, "Lord, You spoke to Abraham and John. You say You change not; You are the same yesterday, today, and forever. [See Hebrews 13:8.] Now is the time to speak out to *me*, Lord; to make Yourself known to me. Lord, I need You to speak in a way I can understand."

Through the drug-induced haze that clouded my senses, my heart clearly heard His response—familiar words from Isaiah 65:24: *"Before you call, I will answer." This is My promise to you, daughter. You are to rely on it and not to anticipate what lies ahead—not even for half an hour.*

In the distance, I heard the footsteps of The Strong Boys. They were coming down the long hall to get me.

"*Lord?!*"

8

Is This Trip Absolutely Necessary?

The Strong Boys pushed my cart into a tremendous square room, brilliant with lights. Swiftly, skillfully, they lifted the corners of my sheet, and before I knew it I was lying on a narrow table. The whole scene seemed unreal—but I lay there in perfect peace, knowing that everything needful would be accomplished.

As I lay under those bright lights waiting for the next development—whatever it was to be—my mind wandered. I remembered reading, soon after I became a Christian, a theory that cancer is caused by bitterness. When I first learned of this theory, I smiled it away. As cases of cancer continually cropped up in my family, however, I began to wonder. My grandmother, my father, and Irvin's father died from the disease. My sister in South Carolina was losing her *long* battle with breast cancer.

If bitterness causes cancer, I thought, *not many members of the human race would escape the disease.* Yet I had never felt that I myself would be a victim. *God, could I be harboring bitterness in my heart and not be aware of it?*

I remembered how much I had suffered in childhood, when my schoolmates made fun of me because I walked with a limp. Were roots of bitterness formed in me at such an early age?

My mind struggled for answers, which would not come. Then gradually the rambling thoughts began to fade; elusive answers no longer seemed important.

During the next few moments something supernatural happened to me. I was suddenly transported from the hospital operating theater into a most marvelous place. Although my body was still lying on the table, I was viewing things on a heavenly plane. I found myself inside a magnificent cathedral—the most beautiful building I had ever seen. It had a white marble dome so huge that it seemed to encompass heaven. The dome was filled with brilliant light. Although my eyes would have been blinded by such brightness, I experienced no discomfort. Indeed, I seemed to become part of the light even while I was standing aside observing it. My joy was boundless.

As I stood within the cathedral looking upward, I saw that something resembling a great, curved, marble disk formed the top of the brilliant dome. The inside walls of the dome were covered with beautiful marble mosaics and carvings, all white and ivory and pulsating with light. The intricately carved moldings were so beautiful that they took my breath.

Gradually, I became aware of children singing, thousands of children, adoring and worshipping God. The music was indescribable—so pure and holy that I knew it was not of earth. I became caught up in it and began praising God aloud with them. It was oh, so beautiful, this music.

"Where is this?" I heard my own voice finally ask the question.

From somewhere, a majestic voice gave me an immediate answer: "You are standing in the house of God."

True to my practical character, I replied, "I didn't know He had a house." Nothing else was said.

I continued to gaze upward, feeling pure and total joy and fully aware of being part of the scene. As the vision gradually faded, I became conscious of a human voice singing aloud, "Lord, I love You; Lord, I praise You; Lord, I worship You."

Opening my eyes, I floated back through clouds to the reality of the sterile operating room. Then I realized that the voice I heard, praising and worshiping God aloud, was mine, and that one arm was lifted up in praise. I fell silent, overwhelmingly aware of the presence of God. He had come down here into the operating room to be with me. Leaving all that heavenly splendor, He had come to stand by me and comfort *me* if I had to hear that most feared word: *cancer.*

But now there was no dread! I had dreaded it in my humanness; but with Jesus here, the dread was gone. I had experienced just a taste of what He must have felt when He was facing the cross: dreading to go through the humiliation and agony, but completely willing for the Father's will to be carried out in His life. That's exactly how I felt now. Although I had no real choice, I was, deep down, so willing to drink any cup of suffering that God saw fit to allow me.

But *was* this God's will? Minutes passed—or was it hours?—and I began to wonder what the doctors were doing. Was the operation over? Why didn't someone tell me something—*any*thing? Did they think I had lost my mind because they heard me singing on the operating table?

Everybody is so quiet. They are all standing around looking down at me. I wonder what they are thinking.

In spite of the Presence hovering near me, the thoughts tumbling about in my mind began to make me feel uneasy. *What am I doing here, when I'm a Christian? I've failed somewhere; this can't be what the Lord wills for my life. He wants good for everyone, not evil. . . . Did He allow this to happen to me—or did I bring it on myself? Was there a way I could have escaped it? There must have been. Lord God, help Me understand. . . .* I knew He would.

Then the Comforter whispered the reminder into my troubled heart: "You are accepted in the Beloved. You are not a failure, because Jesus does not fail. You are a success because He is within you. Joy!" Tears of gratitude filled my eyes, spilling down my cheeks. Such love!

The delay began to seem interminable, the suspense unbearable. Finally, I asked the nurses, "Did you have to remove—?" I never did finish the question, and no one answered it. I tried again: "—all the breast? Someone did say I had cancer, didn't they?" I felt the gentle caress of a nurse's hand. Silence met my question, although I knew people were all around me. Why didn't someone answer me?

Finally, Nurse Oriental-Beauty said, "Dr. Strong-Flower will talk with you in a few minutes." The silence hung in the room, weighing heavily on my heart. No one was talking; they were just moving about. Then, in my heart, I *knew* the answer to my question. But because of the Presence with me, it was all right.

Finally, Dr. Strong-Flower came and completely covered my hand with his. He said simply, "I'm sorry. The biopsy proved you have a malignant tumor. We will have to operate."

"It's all right," I replied. It *was* all right. My Father's presence was still there.

The prick of Dr. Sleep's needle was sharp. For a moment, I felt as if my eyes were rolling around in their sockets. The tremendous lights—very bright now—were all focused on the table where I lay. I don't remember when darkness came; I just remember the light.

9

Learning to Relax

I had left my room on the little wheely cart at 9:15 A.M. Around five o'clock in the afternoon I came back to my room in the same way. The first thing I remember seeing was my husband's concerned face. He forced a weak smile, touching the cart lightly with a pathetic gesture.

"Don't anyone be sad," I said. My own voice startled me. As my eyes and my mind became clearer, I saw that two of my friends, Helen and Mary, were there with my family. They all waited out in the hall while Sturdy Boys carefully transferred me from the cart to the bed. I vaguely remember that, when they came back into the room, it was I who was doing all the talking. Only much later did my friends tell me, with considerable amusement, what I had said.

"You reached over and clutched Tuck's arm," they told me, "and then declared, 'Well, I've decided to live, because there isn't anybody on the face of the earth who can wash as many shirts and socks as I can. . . . Got to take care of my husband's laundry.' With that, you rolled one eyeball one way and one the other and went to sleep. We didn't hear another word from you."

When I awakened the next morning, I discovered that I was attached to two machines, one on either side of the bed. One was pumping "steak and potatoes" (the nurse's description) into my veins. The other seemed to be pumping out my life's blood, quarts at a time—"draining your wound," Dr. Strong-Flower said. I never did understand the process, which continued for many days; but something must have been happening between the intake and the output. My mind wandered up and down, trying to figure out what was going on. I finally gave up and decided simply to trust Hospital Personnel and surrender my body to them. After all, God was in control of my situation and of them, and I trusted *Him*. This decision brought me peace.

I spent most of that first postoperative day lying quietly in bed—thinking, praying, praising God, intermittently singing little snatches of song—just a word or two—to Him in my crackling, weak voice. The praise glorified the Lord and brought healing and comfort to my body. God is good. Never has He failed to honor His promise to inhabit the praises of His people (see Psalm 22:3).

The discovery that I couldn't read my Bible that first day came as a shock. When a person has had a serious operation, lifting a heavy Bible is, for a time, impossible. I had so little strength that I couldn't lift even the small devotional book I had brought with me. Furthermore, I couldn't focus my eyes well enough to read, nor could I tolerate the TV my husband had thoughtfully rented for me. Once again, as on that first night in the hospital, I was made aware of the value of memory. One of the most beautiful things God did for me when I was born again was to give me a love for His Word. I had been storing up Scripture in my mind—not always consciously memorizing it, but going over and over certain treasured passages God had dropped into my heart over the years. By asking the Holy Spirit to seal them unto me, I had made them mine. Now I was gaining a new appreciation of the lasting value of those beautiful verses and "precious promises." Over and over and over again, they were bringing healing, restoration, new life. *His Word never fails me,* I thought gratefully.

When Tuck came into my little room after supper that night, his overcoat was wet and his face rosy red. A cold rain mixed with sleet was falling outside, and I could hear the wind howling. Not knowing what to do to comfort me, Tuck just held my hand. He didn't mention the machines to which I was attached, but acted as if this was a perfectly normal situation.

When Tuck came to see me the second night, I had improved enough to be concerned about his having to drive to the hospital on sleet-slickened streets, find a parking place in the snowy parking lot, and walk to the hospital in the freezing weather. To divert my mind from these anxious thoughts, I suggested that we recite the Twenty-Third Psalm together.

Softly we began, "The Lord is my shepherd; I shall not want. . . ." When we came to the verse about "the valley of the shadow of death," I was made fully aware of the possibility that I might soon have to pass through that valley, and I was not afraid. God had completely taken the fear of death from me, and I knew that if I never got well that would be all right too.

My thoughts went back to the giant marble dome I had seen while I was in the operating room. I knew it was heaven—and because of the peace my Master had given me, I knew heaven must be a wonderful place. So why should I fear death—the portal through which we Christians "enter into the presence of the living God"? *"O death, where is thy sting? O grave, where is thy victory? . . . Thanks be to God, who giveth us the victory through our Lord Jesus Christ"* (1 Corinthians 15:55,57).

With these victorious verses in mind, I fell asleep. When I awakened near midnight, Tuck was gone. The sleet had changed to snow, which was forming interesting little patterns as it blew against the plastic barrier Nurse Glad-Tidings had improvised over my broken window. I sighed. The pain in my arm was so intense that I rang for the nurse and asked her to give me the pain pill I had refused earlier. This request, I felt, was a victory for Satan, since I had determined in my heart that I would trust the Lord for full deliverance from all pain.

As I placed the little white pill on my tongue, I said aloud, "You haven't licked me yet, Satan, and you never will. By His stripes I AM HEALED!" Satan knew I meant it, and that pill was the last narcotic I requested during my entire convalescence. When the pain threatened to overcome me, I quoted Scripture to Satan. Verses from Psalms 98, 100, and 103 were some of my favorite prescriptions for pain. Because God always honors His Word, the "sword of the Spirit" (Ephesians 6:17) is a powerful weapon against Satan. Countless times during the days and nights of my hospitalization, my savings account of Scripture verses delivered me from physical and mental anguish and made intolerable situations tolerable.

It was during one of those well-nigh intolerable situations that God spoke directly to Tuck. He had come by the hospital, as he did every day on his way to the office, to say good morning to me. On this particular morning, Nurse Olympics had just lifted me to a sitting position in the bed and was trying to teach me to raise my almost immobile arm. Tuck walked into my little cubicle just in time to hear me give a loud cry of pain and then see me faint dead away. Bolting from the room, he went into the hall and cried out to God from his whole heart for my healing. This type of prayer did not come easily to one who had never been taught that Jesus died not only for our soul's salvation, but for the salvation of the whole man, including the healing of all our physical infirmities.

When Tuck prayed in this way, the Lord reminded him of the Scriptures from Matthew 8:17 ("Himself took our infirmities, and bare our sicknesses") and Psalm 103:3 ("Who forgiveth all thine iniquities; who healeth all thy diseases"). At that moment He quietly began a new work in my husband's life—a work that led him gradually to a new understanding of what Jesus meant by the question, "Wilt thou be made whole?" (John 5:6).

God was constantly at work bringing good out of everything the enemy put upon us. We were to learn many lessons within the coming months that could have been taught us through no other methods. Had Tuck and I been more spiritually mature or learned the full meaning of Jesus' sacrifice at Calvary on our behalf, perhaps we could have been spared much suffering; but I find that God must take us as individuals where we are in our spiritual walk and guide us into understanding as we are able to learn.

I was on a spiritual journey, taking one step at a time, trusting Him for strength for the next step when the time came for me to take it.

He proved faithful, and I was always able to take that next step successfully. It helped tremendously to constantly repeat the truth, "The blood of Jesus Christ is flowing through my veins every second, bringing new life into my whole being."

As I repeated this truth over and over, five to ten times a day, it brought peace. *I* was at peace.

Since my visitors were restricted, many friends and family members expressed their love by sending flowers. So many arrived that the Pink Ladies had trouble finding places to put them in the tiny room. After the dresser and desk were covered, they placed containers of flowers on the floor under pipes, around the walls, and beneath the lavatory. I loved my "florist shop" and was grateful for each plant or flower arrangement that came.

Lord, You sure did shortchange me with this dinky room, I thought, *but You've made up for it with the flowers.*

Instead of reprimanding me for my complaints, the Father let me know that my gracious acceptance of this small room (even the nurses periodically made remarks about its cramped unattractiveness) could be a witness to my faith in His power to overrule circumstances. I praised the Father for His goodness and gave my wall-to-wall bed a loving pat.

Another lesson the Lord taught me during my hospital stay was a way to cope with the weakness of the flesh by relaxing *totally* within the Father's arms. I did this by mentally throwing all responsibility for my welfare ("casting all my care," 1 Peter 5:7) on Him, knowing that He does indeed care for me. I had heard a popular song about being "laid back in the Father's arms." It brought me comfort to sing snatches of this song and picture myself laid back physically, mentally, emotionally, and spiritually within Jesus' arms. Never before had I experienced such continued peace or known such strength of spirit.

Like Paul, I was learning "in whatsoever state I am, therewith to be content" (Philippians 4:11). Since our feelings are, to some extent, based on decisions, I *chose* to be happy and content, no matter what. I spent most of my waking moments rejoicing—humming and sometimes singing aloud to Jesus. Together with my store of Scripture verses, the old gospel hymns I had learned as a child filled my hours of solitude with contentment. The words came readily to my mind, lifting my spirits and bringing freedom from apprehension about my physical condition. My own composure amazed me.

I realized with gratitude that God hadn't given me merely a *measure* of peace to fill my momentary needs; He had sent the Prince of Peace Himself. My Father is not a dispensary. I don't have to go to Him and say, "Father God, give me peace. Father God, give me hope." Instead, He taught me to say, "Father God, Jesus Christ is the Prince of Peace. He came to live inside me in 1953, when I surrendered my life to Him. I don't have to beg You for peace or anything else, for all that He is I have resident within me forever.

He is my peace. He is my faith. He is my power. All I need do is continually draw upon Him, trust and obey Him, and faithfully feed on the Scriptures." God never wants me to depend on my own resources. Only as I trust in His sufficiency on my behalf am I enabled to face up to whatever comes in life. It is "not by might, nor by power, but by my spirit, saith the Lord of hosts" (Zechariah 4:6).

Although some of the lessons I was learning in the hospital were hard ones, I didn't try to understand why I was in this circumstance or to let any question trouble me for long. I just trusted moment by moment. Then, one memorable day, the Teacher gave me a reward that more than compensated for all my struggle and pain.

10

The Unexpected Visitor

For twenty-five years I had known that Jesus, as the Holy Spirit, lived *within* me. On the day of my surgery, I had felt His presence *beside* me—but He had never manifested Himself to me visibly. I didn't believe in visions and unusual spiritual manifestations from the Lord. I was just a full-blown, active, lifetime Protestant layman, not a Dwight L. Moody or a Smith Wigglesworth.

HOWEVER, one afternoon a few days after my operation, I was lying peacefully in bed, humming softly to myself, when something caused me to look toward the left. At first I felt a presence; Someone was in the room. Then I saw, silhouetted against the wall, the faint outline of a huge, manly figure. It didn't startle me—I don't know why. He was facing the window, which was on the right side of the small room. His head almost touched the ceiling. From His size alone, I could tell this was no ordinary man.

Curious, but not afraid, I kept staring at Him. I was strangely calm—calm enough to wonder why I wasn't terrified at this supernatural intrusion. I was puzzled at my easy acceptance of His presence in my room. There was no fear.

Is this a dream, an illusion? NO! I had had no painkillers for several days. This was actually happening! There really *was* a man, larger than life, in the room with me. His left shoulder seemed to touch the wall dividing the room from the hall. His feet were not visible to me. Strange though it was, His being there did not disturb me; in fact, the whole supernatural scene seemed totally natural.

I thought of the Scripture in the Book of Revelation, "Behold, I stand at the door and knock: if any man hear my voice and open the door, I will come in to him, and will sup with him, and he with me" (3:20). Before, I had always thought that verse was meant for spiritual application only. Now, all my carefully learned doctrine was being adjusted in the twinkling of an eye.

It was an undeniable fact, even to this strong-minded, set-in-her-spiritual-ways Protestant, that Jesus was breaking all my hard-and-fast rules by knocking on my door and coming in to sup and speak with me in His own way. I felt very akin to Paul on the Damascus Road when he asked Jesus, "Who art Thou, Lord?" even though he already knew who was speaking to him.

As I continued to study the massive outline, something familiar about His presence quickened my spirit and my heartbeat. Suddenly I acknowledged the reality of His presence with me. "He is here! He really is here!" Joy flooded my whole being.

"*Jesus*!" I cried aloud. "*I see You*!" As soon as I called His name, the figure became more distinct. Although He did not turn toward me, nor move, He was no longer just in silhouette; now I could see His full form. He was magnificent to look upon!

Elated, I continued to gaze at Him, trying to absorb every detail of His appearance. The first feature that attracted my attention was the richness of His beautiful auburn hair. It was extremely thick and smooth in texture, combed straight back without a part and reaching almost to His shoulders. *It shines as though He gives it a hundred strokes a day,* I thought. Next I noticed the muscular thickness of His right shoulder, which was turned toward me. It looked like that of a man accustomed to manual labor. His arms by His sides, He was standing quietly, as though waiting.

I lay still, just drinking in the overwhelming fact of His presence. Finally, I managed to speak:

"Lord," I asked, "why is it that I don't see any light around You? There is no light around You at all." He gave no reply to this question, and I dared not repeat it.

After a long pause, He said gently, "I'm Jesus Christ, come as your Servant."

Although His voice was not audible, each word was distinct and reached my understanding effortlessly; His words flowed into my deepest being, causing my heart to melt within me. Tears filled my eyes and ran down my face. He still did not move, but continued looking toward the window.

Oh, if I lived forever, I thought, *if I had a million words available to me, I wouldn't be able to describe how I feel at this moment.*

I had never in all my life felt so loved, so desired, so fulfilled, so thoroughly accepted, so safe, so warm, so satisfied. I have been loved all my life—first as a daughter, then as a wife, mother, friend, and Christian sister; I've never been without love. But the love I felt from Jesus at this moment surpassed any love I had ever experienced or could even imagine. Along with His love, He gave me the understanding that everybody in the whole world is loved in this same way.

The tears continued to flow, and I kept wiping them away with a corner of the sheet. Even through the tears, I could still see Him clearly. Something drew my attention to His robe. It was a simple, loose-fitting garment that reached to the floor. Without understanding why, I was so struck with its simplicity that I couldn't stop looking at it.

There must be some particular significance to the robe, I thought, as I noticed the details of its design. Made in a style that servants traditionally wore centuries ago, it had a plain, round neckline, the short opening tied with strings made of the same smoothly woven material as the garment. Something about it reminded me of my hospital gown. Then, to my amazement, I realized that *my gown was whiter than His robe.* In all the pictures of Jesus I had seen, His garments were portrayed as shining white. The robe He was wearing today was a soft gray color.

Suddenly my heart fluttered with excitement. His garment was made of fabric with the very same weave and texture as my hospital gown! Understanding came effortlessly; no words were necessary. I *knew* the significance of His gray robe. He was identifying with *me*!

My Lord had taken upon Himself the role of servant and had come into my hospital room to meet *my* needs! He wanted me to realize that He understood my physical suffering, its resulting mental and emotional anguish—yes, even the groping for spiritual understanding throughout this ordeal. The purity of my white gown represented His righteousness imparted to me when He became my

Savior. With His gray gown, He was showing me that He was taking the lowly place of a servant, as He did for the disciples when He was on earth.

My whole heart seemed to melt with love for Him when I once again recognized the sacrifice He had made for me at Calvary. Tears flowed down my cheeks, and this time I made no effort to wipe them away.

Still facing the window, He spoke again: "I am thoroughly and totally one with you in this circumstance, My child."

I thought my heart would burst with the love I had for Him, and with the knowledge of His love for me. He asked me if I remembered the verse He had given me before my operation.

"Yes, Lord," I replied. "You promised that before I called, You would answer" (see Isaiah 65:24).

He smiled and said, "I give you another—not to replace that one, but rather to reinforce it: 'Fear not, daughter of Zion: behold, thy King cometh' " (John 12:15). Then He was gone.

As I lay gazing toward the wall where He had been, I suddenly felt lonelier than I had ever felt in all my life. Sobbing like a small, brokenhearted child, I called after Him, "Please come back, Jesus. Please don't leave me. *Please* come back!" But the Presence was gone. Except for me, the room was now empty.

Inconsolable, I wept as though my heart would break. How could I know what He meant by those words, "Fear not, daughter of Zion"? Was I still afraid? I didn't *feel* afraid. And what did He mean when He said, "Behold, thy King cometh"? Would I actually see Him again with my physical eyes?

At this new thought, my heart began to sing. Drying my tears, I hugged the experience to myself as I sang aloud in the stark hospital room a song I had learned as a joyful little child:

> And He walks with me, and He talks with me,
> And He tells me I am His own,
> And the joy we share as we tarry there,
> None other has ever known.[1]

Now, for the very first time in my life, I understood what the song really means.

---

[1] "In the Garden," by C. Austin Miles, copyright © 1912 by Hall-Mack Co., copyright renewed, 1940, by Homer Rodeheaver.

At that moment, Nurse Checkup pushed the door open and was inside my room before I knew it. She looked alarmed when she saw my tearstained face.

"What's the matter?" she asked with genuine concern.

"I'm just singing," I replied. "I'm okay." I tried to make my voice sound normal.

She gave me a strange look, but finally turned away and reached for the thermometer on the bedside table. As she put it in my mouth, I wondered what the reading would be. I had just had an audience with the King!

As the afternoon wore on, I became very restless. Would supper ever be over and the visitors allowed to come upstairs? I could hardly wait for Tuck to get there, so that I could tell him about my visit from Jesus. I barely touched my meal.

It was later than usual when I heard Tuck's quick step in the hall. He came in with snow on his overcoat and his hat pulled down over his eyes. His glasses were wet, and his face was ruddy from the cold. Not waiting for him to say a single word, I greeted him excitedly: "Oh, Tuck, I've got something to tell you!"

He pulled off his snow-covered overcoat, shook it vigorously, then folded it carefully and put it on the desk, with his soaking hat on top of it. Coming over to my bed, he planted a wet kiss on my forehead and sat down without saying anything.

Rushing on, I told him all about my Visitor, giving a full description with complete details. Like a wound-up phonograph, I continued talking until I had run down. When I finally lay back on my pillow, I realized for the first time that Tuck still had not said a word. He sat looking down toward the floor, obviously not sharing my excitement.

"What's the matter?" I asked, disappointment in my tone. At the moment, I was totally unmindful of the hardships my husband was enduring because of my sickness, and of the toll it was taking on him, both emotionally and physically. I had been thinking only of the way it was affecting *me*.

I knew Tuck found it difficult to believe in visions—and so did I. Although I had heard stories about others seeing Jesus, I never believed they were true. Supernatural visitations were commonplace in the Bible, I knew—but they didn't happen today! Until my experience that afternoon, it would have been unthinkable. Had I been in Tuck's place, I don't know that I could have accepted my account either.

"Helen," Tuck finally said, "you don't realize how difficult it is to get a parking space in that crowded lot, in all this snow, at this time of night."

I was dumbfounded. Such an unappreciative response! I had been waiting all evening to share my glorious experience with Tuck. My mind just couldn't take in his lack of enthusiasm, or even *interest*.

"Well, I realize it's hard for you to accept," I began, "but—"

"The temperature's almost zero," Tuck interrupted, "and I don't even know whether I can get the car back up the hill to the house." His voice continued in a monotone as I stopped listening.

Lord, what's the matter? I whispered down in my heart. Silence. I asked again: *Lord, what's the matter?*

Just love him. It was the Lord's sweet voice.

Turning my head toward my husband, I saw his face in the glare of the overhead light. He looked extremely tired and pale, his face lined with concern and fatigue. My heart, suddenly saddened, grieved for him.

God, forgive me, I prayed. *Help me to show Tuck understanding.*

Then I said gently, "Tuck, guess who loves you!"

His weary face softened as he turned toward me. Rising from his chair, he pulled it close to my bed and sat down beside me.

I understood.

My husband wasn't really indifferent toward me, just extremely weary. He laid his head on the bed beside my pillow and closed his eyes. Again we were at peace.

After Tuck had left and I was snuggling down under the covers, ready for sleep, I heard the Lord speak, way down inside my heart. *Behold, your King came! I loved you through Tuck. Learn to recognize love's vestments, daughter; your husband is clothed with them too.*

My tears flowed onto the pillow. Now I was beginning to understand the meaning of the promise He had given me that afternoon: "Behold, your King cometh." He wanted me to recognize Him in anyone who came to me out of love, as Tuck had done that night.

O Lord, I have so much to learn, I thought. *Thank You for being such a merciful, patient Teacher.*

I wasn't prepared for His next words: *Be patient with* yourself, *daughter.*

Such reassurance—such love! No condemnation, just acceptance of my human frailties.

What a God!

11

Walking—but Not Leaping

"Today, we will unhook one machine, and tomorrow you will get up." It was Dr. Strong-Flower speaking to me. "Every time you get out of bed, turn off the blood-pumping machine. You must remember—never, never, never are you to forget—to turn that machine back on *as soon as* you get back into bed, *every* time."

I looked at him in disbelief. I couldn't imagine ever being able to rise up off that bed, much less to turn the knobs that controlled the machine. But if he said I was to do it, then I knew I would soon be up and walking around. One of the things I had learned about Dr. Strong-Flower was that his word was his bond.

On the day after my operation, I had learned something else about his word: *It carried authority in the hospital.* One of the machines I was hooked up to was exceptionally noisy. Apparently everyone on the hall was being driven to distraction by its "pump-pump-pump." On that first postoperative day, I heard Dr. Strong-Flower speak softly to the head nurse, asking her to have the machine removed and replaced with another one. When he came in to see me the next day, the machine was still there. This time he spoke sharply, though still quietly, to Head Nurse, telling her that he did *not* want to find that noisy machine in the room on his next visit.

"I don't believe we have another one," she replied.

"There *are* other machines." The authority in his voice was unmistakable. "And this one had better not be here when I come back. If she wasn't already sick, that machine would *make* her sick. It will not be in this room tomorrow!"

Head Nurse vanished immediately, and shortly behind her starched white figure the machine also vanished—to be replaced by a much smaller, quieter model.

From that experience, I learned what the nurses already knew: that Dr. Strong-Flower's overriding concern was for the welfare of his patients, and that he would go to any length to see that they received the best treatment the hospital could afford. Again I thanked my God and my Father that He had picked this man to be my surgeon.

This afternoon, Dr. Strong-Flower's concern for my welfare was causing him to demand the impossible from me. He showed me how to turn off a knob controlling each tube that connected my body to the pumping machine, and how to plug the tubes with plastic caps. After I had done that, he said, I was to put the tubes in my bathrobe pocket, get out of bed, and walk down the hall. This routine was to be carried out morning and afternoon.

"I don't mean to treat you like a child," he said, "but I'd like to see you turn off the machine twice before I leave."

I got an A-plus on this exam. With Dr. Strong-Flower standing over me, it was easy enough—but I didn't know what I would do when he left and I actually had to get out of bed after going through this complicated maneuver. It seemed incomprehensible that I would be able to turn off a machine that was keeping me going, *then* put on my own bathrobe and slippers and walk down the hall without help.

I was already having a hard enough time performing my arm-raising ceremony. Dr. Strong-Flower had told me that I *must* lift my arm back over my head ten times a day, or I would lose the use of it. In the face of this alternative I obeyed, in spite of the physical and emotional torture involved.

So many chest and underarm muscles had been removed that the arm had little support. Often I would have the panicky feeling that, once I had gone through the agony of lifting my arm over my head, I would never be able to get it back down. My body was unbalanced, and my arm felt out of control—almost like a screen door with a broken spring. We once had such a door—and when the wind blew, it would come open and bang wildly until someone went down the steps, grasped the little handle, and latched it shut. I felt that my arm also needed a handle I could grasp, in order to pull it back to safety.

The morning after Dr. Strong-Flower gave me my marching orders, in came a nurse with an expression that said, "I'd do it all for you, except I know I can't get away with it." From her face, I knew she had a kind heart.

"You must be a Christian," was my greeting to her.

She smiled and replied, "Yes, I am."

"Oh, that's marvelous!" I exclaimed.

"It may be marvelous," she said, "but it's not going to keep you from getting out of that bed."

This ultimatum was delivered with a big grin and a twinkle in her bright green eyes. Instantly, I made up my mind to cooperate if it killed me. *And it probably will,* I thought, steeling myself for the inevitable.

Nurse Christian, aided and abetted by a hefty nurse who had followed her into the room, unhooked me from the machine. (They didn't ask me to do it alone the first few times.) Then Big Nurse got on one side of the bed and Nurse Christian on the other. "Roll over!" they ordered.

I said aloud, "O Lord, help!" It was one of the hardest things I had ever been forced to do, but somehow I did roll over to the edge of the bed. Nurse Christian knew just how to manage me. Offering me her arm, she said, "Grab hold."

"With what?" I asked.

"Well, with whatever you have to grab hold with."

Somehow I managed to grab Nurse Christian's elbow with my good arm, and she and Big Nurse eased me up to a sitting position, with my legs dangling off the side of the bed. It wasn't as painful as I had feared it would be. Big Nurse put a little rubber-capped stool under my feet; then they lifted me gently off the bed, one nurse on either side of me.

I cautiously put one foot on the floor, then the other. Then I fainted. The next thing I remember was being back in the familiar bed with the little machine going "blump-blump-blump." I felt weak but safe.

I heard no more about walking *that* day. But the next morning, bright and early, Nurse Alert came into my room and announced cheerfully, "You are getting out of bed today!" Her voice lifted sing-song. When I saw that she was followed by Nurse Helper, my heart sank—for I knew she meant *now*.

O Lord! Up went my plea for help.

An attendant on either side of me, I repeated the procedure of the day before—including the faint. Then I was back in bed: "blump-blump-blump."

When Dr. Strong-Flower made his evening rounds, he was understanding and encouraging, but relentless in his determination that I walk. "It sounds very normal to me," he said. "Same thing tomorrow, same time."

I knew then that eventually I was going to have to get out of bed and *walk*. I carried the dread of tomorrow's ordeal into my sleep.

During the night, the Lord reminded me of a wonderful promise He had made to me on the day of my surgery. As I was coming out of the anesthesia, somewhere deep down in me was the knowledge that I was not to anticipate for even half an hour what lay ahead. When the time came, He would give me victory, regardless of what I had to endure. It was the Prince of Peace who gave me that promise, and now He was reminding me of it to strengthen me when I needed it.

The next morning, when The Nurse Patrol came in to help me get off the machine and out of bed, one foot went down on the floor; the other foot went down beside it—and I crept cautiously to the chair! Everyone grinned. Everyone was happy, especially me.

Satisfied for the moment, they helped me get back in bed, hooked me up to the machine, and marched out in formation. That afternoon, as if on cue, they marched back in. This time I walked to the door. Again, everybody rejoiced; then out they went.

After that, there was no denying Dr. Strong-Flower's marching orders. Every day, twice a day, after The Patrol had unhooked the machine and helped me out of bed, I was off down the hall in my rosy-red bathrobe—quaking and shaking and holding to the wall, but still walking in victory.

Then came the day when I had to carry out the total procedure with no help from Hospital Personnel. With trembling hands, I unhooked myself from the machine, carefully turned it off and capped the tubes, put on my robe and slippers. I kept reminding myself, *I am complete in Him; I am complete in Him* (see Colossians 2:10). Then I began teeter-tottering down the hall.

I was shocked by the imbalance of my body! It kept pulling me to one side; I felt out of control, gripped by momentary panic. *What to do? Not a familiar face in sight.*

Out of my memory bank came the promise from Romans 8:37: "We are more than conquerors through him that loved us." Reminding myself that He was with me, I again began creeping along the wall, grasping the handrail as if my very life depended upon its stability. I kept praying that no one would pass near and push me off balance, causing me to falter and fall. With every step I took, I reminded the Lord, *I'm walking by faith and not by sight* (see 2 Corinthians 5:7). I wanted Him to be on the alert to catch me if I fell.

When I finally made it back to my door, exhausted but exhilarated, I felt as though Mount Everest had been conquered. I had finally completed the whole procedure—unaided except for my Savior!

Trembling from the effort, I got back in bed, reconnected myself to the machine, and settled down. Again, He had proved to be sufficient for my need. Promise after promise from the Scripture came to my mind: "My strength is made perfect in weakness" (2 Corinthians 12:9); "The joy of the Lord is your strength" (Nehemiah 8:10); "Casting all your care upon him; for he careth for you" (1 Peter 5:7); "Thanks be to God, which giveth us the victory through our Lord Jesus Christ" (1 Corinthians 15:57).

Then Jesus began to give me some thoughts. He told me to learn to *pray* the verses appropriate for any particular situation. *Claim them, rely on them, repeat them to yourself over and over until the truth of each promise becomes real to you. Cast down "imaginations, and every high thing that exalts itself against the knowledge of God"* (see 2 Corinthians 10:5).

Don't accept fear thoughts. Defeat them with the promises of God that apply to your need of the moment. "Look not at the things which are seen, but at the things which are not seen" (2 Corinthians 4:18).

"Faith cometh by hearing, and hearing by the word of God" (Romans 10:17). *Learn to meditate upon the Word. Think deeply about each verse. Ask Me, and I will show you great and mighty truths peculiar to your present need. Meditation in the Word brings*

tremendous benefits and marvelous blessings. Learn to practice it. Remember I said: "Come unto me, all ye that labour and are heavy laden, and I will give you rest. Take my yoke upon you, and learn of me. . . . For my yoke is easy, and my burden is light" (Matthew 11:28–30).

Get into my yoke beside Me. Let My strength lift the burden. See, I am here. I never leave or forsake you. Count on Me. Take note of what My words promise you. Pause and think upon what they are holding out to you. Take from Me everything you need. You can always count on Me.

Then He said to my listening heart: *See how important it has been for you to memorize the Scripture over the years? Before you call, I answer, if you are open to Me* (see Isaiah 65:24). *That is why I say to memorize the Word of God, so that it will become one with you. And learn of Me, learn of Me, learn of Me. Then you will find rest for your soul.*

I lay quiet for a long time, thinking about what He had said. Then my thoughts returned to my walk of triumph. I felt like a student pilot who has just completed his first solo flight. I was eager to try my wings in new territory. My Teacher hadn't told me that He had made out flight plans in advance.

12

HPT Delivery Service

As long as the antiquated pumping machine was going, I wasn't aware of noises in the hall; but when it was replaced by a quieter one, I could hear a constant flow of discordant sounds coming from the room directly across from me. A woman with a foreign accent kept calling the nurses. No matter how often they came, she would demand their return as soon as they left. Whatever was wrong with her, it had not weakened her vocal cords! If the nurses didn't feed her and wait on her like a baby, she complained and harassed them; yet I never heard one of the nurses speak to her in an unkind tone.

Although I hadn't seen this woman, she was often on my mind. One day, as I was praying for her, I asked the Lord to show me what her problem was and what I could do to help her.

Her problem, He told me, was that she didn't feel loved or wanted by any human being in the world. He showed me that she was like a little cast-off puppy that was yelping and crying because it was starved for attention and affection.

I began to pray for her in earnest. Then one day Friend Dottie came in to visit me, smiling broadly and carrying a beautiful lavender box from the florist. She opened it for me, disclosing six perfect sweetheart rosebuds arranged as a pillow corsage. Oh, I loved it and was so proud of it! Dottie and I decided the best place to put it was on the window curtain. Maybe it would draw attention away from the frayed edges of the plastic shield Nurse Glad-Tidings had put over the window to cover the broken pane. Dottie carefully pinned the corsage on the curtain, right in my line of vision.

The next morning, the first thing I saw when I opened my eyes was those lovely rosebuds. And the first thing I heard, when I opened my heart to the Lord, was this astounding request: *Helen, I want you to give that corsage to the woman across the hall.*

I protested weakly: *But, Lord, how am I going to take that thing down and get it over to her?*

He knew the problem wasn't just the physical effort involved but the giving up of my flowers—reminders of a friend who loved me enough to brave the sleet and slush outside to deliver them personally.

Helen, get the box. The voice within was loving but firm.

I was sure the box had been thrown away in the trash—but I was wrong. It had somehow fallen out of the trash basket, and when Nurse's Aide Step-n-Fetchit made her rounds, she found it under the desk. At my request, she retrieved it for me and removed the corsage from the curtain. I nestled it tenderly into the green waxed paper still inside the box. It looked as though it had just come from the florist: fresh, pink, and beautiful. Oh, I did hate to give it up!

I cut off the machine and got out of bed. After putting on my bathrobe and picking up the florist's box, I walked across the hall and entered The Lady's room just as her daughter-in-law arrived for a visit. I introduced myself and handed the box to the visitor, saying that I wanted her mother-in-law to have the flowers. Although I stayed only a few moments, I could sense the love of Jesus flowing around the three of us while the younger woman and I were talking. The patient didn't say a word, but her eyes never left my face, except for a quick glance at the flowers.

From that day until The Lady left the hospital, I never heard her speak sharply to another nurse. No more moans or complaints came from her room. The Lord explained to me that this change had taken place because The Lady received His love through the gift of flowers.

At that time I didn't know how many lives would be changed through the love God had me share with other patients—or how He would bless my own life as I was obedient to His directions.

One day the Lord took me by a room in which a black grandmother, tall, thin and beautiful, lay propped up on pillows. Something about her lovely face drew me into the room. After I had introduced myself, she introduced her teenage son and married daughter. We exchanged pleasantries, and I gave them several of the gospel tracts I always carried around in my bathrobe pockets. Then I returned to my room.

A day or so later, God said to me, *Get up and go take The Grandmother that bouquet of spring flowers.* I knew He meant the handsome arrangement of narcissi and tulips that had arrived just the day before. Their fragrance permeated my little room, constantly drawing my attention to their beauty.

Lord, I grumbled, *I'll lose every friend I have if I keep this up. As fast as these flowers come in, You send me around with them like the FTD service. What will my friends think when they come to visit me and don't see their flowers in my room?*

There was no reply from the Lord, but it was clear that He hadn't changed His mind. Still protesting inwardly, I reluctantly climbed out of bed and picked up the flowers, balancing them against my side. Shaking from the exertion, I walked down the hall, somehow managing to hold the handrail without dropping the flowers.

"I brought you something!" I said as I entered The Grandmother's room. Her brown eyes shone with pleasure as they watched the transfer of the bouquet from my arm to her bedside table. Although she did not acknowledge the flowers or form the words, "Thank you," I knew that from the bottom of her heart she reached out to me with gratitude.

It wasn't long before my new friend paid me a return visit. As we were talking, she told me that a cancer had been removed from her stomach four years earlier and that she had entered the hospital to find the reason for a recurrence of pain in that area. Putting her hand on her left side, she remarked without much conviction, "The doctors say it might be just muscular."

"Let's pray about it," I suggested. I don't remember the words that came forth, but they were brief. When the prayer was finished, I asked her to come over to the bed so that I could pat her beautiful face. I couldn't hug her because of the tubes in my arm, but she pressed her cheek against mine as we said good-bye.

"I was so lonely; then you came," she whispered into my ear. "The good Lord sent you." Before I could answer, she was gone.

A few days later, I went past her room on my morning walk. She called out to me, "I've got something to tell you."

"What is it?" I asked, walking over to her bed.

"I want you to pray for the other side like you did for this one," she replied. "The pain there is all gone."

Oh, how I rejoiced! And how confidently I prayed for her right side, just as the Lord had had me pray for her left side. Then I said, "Come to see me soon."

She came to my room the very next afternoon, joy written all over her face. She wanted to tell me that the doctors had dismissed her and she was going home the next day. They had found no evidence that her cancer had returned.

As we rejoiced together, I heard the Lord say, *Give her the potted plant to take home with her.*

Which one, Lord?

The big one. That one was from Friend Jackie, and I wanted to replant it at home.

Well, Lord, I argued, *there are two just alike. . . .*

I said, "The big *one."*

When I showed The Grandmother the larger of the two plants and told her I wanted her to have it, she said, "You know, I got one just like this two years ago, when my husband died. Ain't had anything like it since. I live in a trailer by myself and I work for my living. How can I thank you?"

"Just by praying for me," I answered. As we looked at each other, my heart seemed to turn over with love for her. She nodded her head toward me and, without another word, took the plant and shuffled out in her worn bedroom shoes.

What if I had denied her the larger plant? O Lord, make me unselfish and grateful! I still secretly hoped He wouldn't ask me to share any of the flowers from Tuck or our two sons or my beloved daughter-in-law. *Forgive my selfishness, Lord,* I prayed, *but my family means so much to me. May I please keep* their *gifts?*

The next day, hearing voices and the sound of a wheelchair coming down the hall, I turned my head toward the open door. There was that dear grandmother, sitting straight up in the chair like royalty, one arm wrapped around the potted plant and the other around the vase of now-dried-up spring flowers. She looked neither to the right nor to the left, until, just as she passed, she glanced toward my open door and nodded her head stiffly from the neck up.

Then she was gone. From where I lay, I could see the Lord's victory on her face.

His love had worked its miracle in another life, and He had allowed me to catch a glimpse of it.

With this scene constantly in mind, I began to share my flowers freely with patients in the wards and in private rooms—even with the nurses at the nursing station. It seemed that the more flowers I gave away, the more came in to me. And never once did the Lord ask me to part with the gifts from my precious family. Truly, God *is* Love!

13
Patricia

Somewhere around the eighth day after my operation—I had lost track of time—I gradually became aware that I was beginning to feel like a human being once again. Having learned to take a few steps without wobbling, I felt victorious, even happy, as I lay in bed one morning, talking to the Lord. Though my physical body was weak, the "inner woman" felt strong.

Suddenly I heard Him say, *Get up and go down the hall. I have something for you to do.*

Now, Lord? I hoped He'd say, *Later.* Moving around was such a hassle.

Yes, now.

I was reminded of another Scripture: "And when he putteth forth his own sheep, he goeth before them, and the sheep follow him; for they know his voice" (John 10:4). I would need this verse very badly in a few minutes, though I didn't know it then.

With reluctant obedience, I unhooked myself from the machine, twisted the knobs, capped the tubes, and put them in the pockets of my bathrobe. Not knowing where I was going, and hearing footsteps behind me, I stopped, leaned against the wall, and let the owner of the feet go around me. I was so weak and my body felt so badly out of balance that I didn't dare let go of the handrail that ran the length of the corridor.

At the end of the hall, I received an uncertain mental signal, *Straight ahead.* Jesus said that His sheep would know His voice (see John 10:4), and I knew that the voice I had heard was not the voice of the Good Shepherd. The enemy was trying to sidetrack me by leading me into the men's ward. I paused for a few seconds, listening; then I heard the sweet voice of Jesus say, *Turn right. DON'T RUSH. TRUST.*

I turned to the right and walked down that hall, all the way to the little sunroom at the end. When I got there, I knew in my heart that I was in the right place, even though the room was full and there was no seat for me. Soon a patient got up and went out, leaving a place on the sofa. I sat down beside an elderly gentleman and waited for further directions. One by one, the patients who had been in the room got up and left. Finally, only one remained—a precious young woman who appeared to be in her late twenties. She had short black hair and wore a velveteen bathrobe, royal blue trimmed with white lace; it had a little hood in the back that bounced up and down when she moved. My heart was touched by her restless movements and by her look of youthful vulnerability. I walked over and sat down beside her. After a few minutes, I reached out and touched her lightly on the arm.

"How're you doing?" I asked with a smile.

Wide green eyes turned to look straight at me. "I'm so afraid!" The words seemed to burst from her lips. Her little body was trembling noticeably, and she kept twisting the corner of her robe with nervous fingers.

"What's the matter, honey?" I asked gently, my voice low.

"I'm so afraid," she repeated. "They operated on me last Wednesday, but I'm still afraid." The robe-twisting ritual took on added fervor.

"Why are you still afraid?"

"Because I know that, if I had died on that operating table, I would have gone to hell."

The bluntness of her words startled me—but only for a moment. They made it clear that the Master was about His business.

"But you *didn't* die," I pointed out. "God didn't let you."

She looked at me as if embarrassed. The nervous twisting stopped, and she began stroking the velveteen robe as if caressing it.

"I've never been to church," she told me wistfully. She paused, then continued, "I've never even been inside a church." Now the words came with a rush. "Have you ever met anyone who hasn't even seen the inside of a church? I mean, not *ever*?"

I could tell that the question had been bottled up inside her for a long time.

"That's all right," I reassured her. "That's not the important thing."

Neither of us had mentioned Jesus by name; I was waiting for the prompting of the Holy Spirit.

Now she went back to the subject of her surgery. "I had a hysterectomy, and it still hurts. Do you reckon I'll be all right?"

Her face was turned toward me, as though she was expecting something. So I began telling her about the Savior, a wonderful man named Jesus, who had come to forgive us and to take our sins away, making us as though we had never sinned. He could wipe out her past, I told her, and give her a brand-new beginning. He came to seek and to save those who are lost; to *heal* and redeem body, soul, and spirit; to make us completely whole.

"Can He keep me from being scared anymore?" she asked—so I told her how He had taken away my fear of the swinging doors leading to the operating room. Tears formed in her eyes as she listened, and I could sense that her heart was absorbing every word.

"Nobody ever told me about Jesus before," she said. "No man or woman ever told me about Him. Can you believe that?" She wiped her eyes with the back of her hand.

Smiling, I said, "Let me tell you about a healing." I spent a few minutes talking to her about my inability to have a second child until God healed my body. Then I asked her, "Wouldn't you like to receive the Lord Jesus into your heart to become your Savior—to make you every bit whole?"

"No!" she replied, and drew back, trembling even more.

I waited silently. *Lord, what do I do now?* I patted her hand gently, then rose and crossed to the other side of the room. I didn't want to rush her out of the Kingdom of God. I had done that to others in the past. Picking up a magazine, I sat down on a sofa near her chair and began leafing through the pages, stealing an occasional glance at her wistful face. Soon I saw her eyes fill with tears. Furtively, she wiped them away.

"Honey, what's your name?" I held out my one good arm toward her. Suddenly, she rose from her chair, came over to the sofa, and sat down beside me.

"Patricia," she sobbed. With that, she gave up all pretense of self-control. Tears flowed unchecked as the Lord did His work in her heart. I could do nothing except hand her tissues and pat her shoulder now and then.

When her tears finally subsided a bit, I asked, "Patricia, would you like to pray a little prayer and ask Jesus to come into your life, to be your Lord and Savior, and to make His home with you? He'll take away all your sins, *and* all your fears. He'll bring healing to your body and to your emotions. He's the Prince of Peace. He'll wrap His arms around you and let you *know* that you are forgiven. You won't be afraid anymore. He will never leave you or forsake you."

Turning her tear-stained face to me, she smiled. "Yes, ma'am," she replied shyly. "I *would* like to pray that prayer."

Before leading her in the sinner's prayer, I drew from my memory bank the message of John 3:16. "God loved the world (and Patricia) so much," I told her, "that He sent His only Son, Jesus, to earth to keep us from going to hell and to give us eternal life with Him." Then, paraphrasing Romans 10:9, I said to her, "If you will confess with your mouth that Jesus is your Lord, and if you believe in your heart that God raised Him from the dead, you will be saved. The Bible says that 'with the heart man believeth unto righteousness; and with the mouth confession is made unto salvation. . . . For whosoever shall call upon the name of the Lord shall be saved' " (Romans 10:10, 13).

After that, Patricia and I prayed the sinner's prayer together. She repeated it after me, line by line, speaking each word carefully and deliberately: "Lord Jesus, I am sorry for my sins. Please forgive me. I receive You as my Lord and Savior. Take control of my life and make me the person You want me to be. Thank You for saving me. In Jesus' name. Amen."

There in the hospital sunroom, she accepted Jesus as her Lord and Savior.

"Thank You, O Lord Jesus," I prayed aloud. "Now, please come and wrap Your arms around this young woman and draw her to Yourself. Lord, when we were without strength, You came and gave us *Your* strength. You promised that in our weakness You would be our supreme strength—and O God, we thank You!"

Together, we walked down the hall to Patricia's room, supporting each other and thanking the Lord for what He had done in her life. When we got to her door, I left her and walked back to my room. Joyful but exhausted, I climbed into bed, reconnected the tubes, and turned the knobs that started the machine pumping.

O Lord, how I love You! And how I thank You that You will continue the good work You've begun in Patricia's heart!

Softly, I began humming "At the cross, at the cross . . ." to the accompaniment of the suddenly sweet sounds of the *blump, blump, blumping* machine. Soon I was asleep.

14

"Where Will We Go Tomorrow?"

When I opened my eyes the next morning, the first thought that came to my mind was Patricia. *Lord, she doesn't have a Bible. Someone needs to get one for her. Somebody has to nurture her, strengthen her, start her reading the Bible.*

The Lord's instruction came to me: *Lie still.*

But Lord, I've got to get out of this bed and help her.

This time God was more emphatic. "*Lie still,*" *I said. I don't need you.*

Lord? Then I remembered that in Corinth it was Paul who planted, but Apollos who watered the seeds Paul had planted. *Yes, Lord, and I remember that You are the one who gave the increase.* (See 1 Corinthians 3:6.) I smiled, content.

The following day I felt the Spirit prompting me to go down to Patricia's room. I found her propped up in bed, looking so young, eager, and full of New Life that my heart almost burst with maternal pride. Putting my good arm around her and giving her half a hug, I said, "If I had to come to this hospital just to introduce you to Jesus, it would have been worth it. Do you know that, girl? I love you because Jesus loves you."

She looked back at me with all the understanding of the Kingdom. "I know it," she replied. Then, like an excited child, she said to me, "Guess what I found!"

"What?"

"I found a Bible!"

My heart leaped.

"Come on, I'll show you where it is. I *couldn't* just steal it."

In my heart, I felt that she was hoping I *would* "just steal it" for her. I might have been tempted to do so, if I had thought that was the only way to get a Bible to her immediately. But I knew my God had a better plan.

Patricia led me into a ward and showed me a little blue Testament lying on a dresser. But it didn't belong to either of us.

"It has the hospital name stamped on it," Patricia whispered, "so I'm sure it will be all right if we borrow it. Nobody else is using it."

Her eagerness to read God's Word propelled me into action. In the bed next to the dresser lay a dear old woman who was obviously closer to heaven than she was to earth. I laid my hand over her thin, blue-veined one and said to her, "We'd like to borrow this New Testament, but we'll bring it back. Is that all right?"

Although she didn't answer, she turned her head and looked at me in a way that made me think of my own mother just before she too stepped across the boundary separating heaven from earth. I felt Jesus' Spirit within me pouring His love out on her. Knowing that she felt it too, I asked her if she'd like me to pray with her. When she nodded her consent, I prayed a short prayer, asking the Father to let her *feel* His everlasting arms beneath her and about her. Then I took the Testament from the dresser and handed it to Patricia. We tiptoed out of the ward, rejoicing. When I left her in her room, she was lying on the bed, squeezing the Bible between her hands in utter delight.

"I'll see you tomorrow," I promised.

It was hard to make myself walk slowly down the hall to Room 321. My heart was so full of joy that I longed to skip like a child.

When I walked into Patricia's room the next morning, she squealed and struggled out of bed. Hobbling over to me, she took my good hand in both of hers. The little hood on the back of her robe danced up and down.

"Guess what! Guess what!" she exclaimed exultantly. "A Baptist minister from my hometown came to see me after you left, and brought me a Bible!" She gave the full details—assuring me that she had returned the borrowed New Testament to its proper place. It was plain to see that Patricia was delighted with her newfound Lord and with her new, very own Bible. From way down deep inside me, I heard the Lord say, *Thank you, My daughter. You planted, the minister watered, and I gave the increase.*

After Patricia and I had talked a little while, I kissed her cheek and went back to my bed. When I had reconnected myself to the machine, I settled back to spend some time praising God for saving Patricia's soul.

You are learning the true value of obedience, daughter.

Sir? I was surprised to have Him interrupt the praise.

Ignoring my surprise, He continued. *This is important. Listen closely. In any situation, think not what you are capable of doing or what you know. Think only of who I am.*

The Lord then began explaining to me the importance of my obedience concerning Patricia. *The day before yesterday you wanted to get her a Bible immediately. Had you gone back to her room at that moment, you would have prevented the blessing I wanted her to have. Left alone, she was made to feel her need for the Word. When she acted on her faith and found a Bible for herself, her faith was greatly strengthened. Then the minister I sent to her was able to establish a lasting relationship for Me. Because you were obedient when I told you to stay away, I was able to accomplish much for Patricia's future, when you won't be there to help her.*

I was elated—not only because of what God had done for Patricia, but because He had actually *thanked* me for being obedient! What a Savior!

After coping with my lunch and taking a short afternoon hall-walk, I lay in bed meditating on all the Lord had taught me that day. As afternoon passed swiftly into early evening, shadows filled the room, melting everything into sameness. The supper tray was delivered and taken away, untouched. Nurses came and went. Lost in deep meditation, I was so oblivious of the passing of time that Tuck's nightly visit after supper took me by surprise. Mistaking my abstraction for fatigue and being fatigued himself, he left earlier than usual.

When he had gone and the usual bedtime routine was completed, I turned off the light over my bed and went back to my meditation.

Before long, a verse of Scripture came into my consciousness: "The cup which my Father hath given me, shall I not drink it?" (John 18:11). I lay very still, waiting. . . . The words came again, this time more insistently: "The cup which my Father hath given me, shall I not drink it?" I knew that Jesus, by His own choice, drank the cup of suffering on the cross in order to give us eternal life. *But—did I ever* have *a choice about my anguish and pain*?

The question popped into my mind, taking me by surprise. Immediately, it was replaced by a verse from my Scripture memory bank: "I want to know Christ and the power of his resurrection and the *fellowship of sharing in his sufferings,* becoming like him in his death" (Philippians 3:10 NIV, italics added). It brought instant comfort. Then, remembering that the Scripture I had been concentrating on was a sentence spoken by Jesus in the Garden of Gethsemane just before He was betrayed by Judas, I felt a sudden stab of shame. *O Lord, please wash away all self-pity and any hidden resentment. "Create in me a clean heart, O God; and renew a right spirit within me*" (Psalm 51:10).

I repeated the verse over and over in my mind, prayerfully meditating on each word. Then as I remained alert, waiting, my inner ear heard His unmistakable voice saying to me, *Obedience is the rare thing for which I am seeking today.*

Yes, Lord. Forgive me, Jesus. Instantly the shame vanished. A forgiving God knew and understood my human heart. How I longed to please Him! *But it takes a lifetime to be molded into His image,* I reminded myself.

His voice continued speaking to my heart: *Do you want to know more about obedience, daughter?*

Lord, You know I do. But can't You teach me some way other than through suffering? Isn't there a better way, Lord? Am I so strong-willed, so stubborn that I can't learn any other way? Jesus, surely it isn't so!

I pleaded with Him in my spirit. *Lord, why can't the Holy Spirit just* teach *me what I need to know? Must I,* all my lifetime, *continue to suffer in order to learn*? The questions spilled from my heart as fast as the tears from my eyes. *Lord, I'm* tired *of suffering—mentally, physically, emotionally—the whole thing. I'm weary and worn, God. Please show me the way of obedience without suffering.* Now I was crying aloud to God, the tears having turned into deep sobs.

Suddenly I realized that I had taken the conversational ball away from Jesus and run with it. After asking and receiving His forgiveness for the self-pity revealed by an earlier question, I had immediately launched into an outburst of "murmuring," letting the pronoun *I* monopolize the conversation begun by my Lord.

Sorrowful in my spirit, I whispered into the darkness, "Forgive me, Lord." Painfully I adjusted the pillow under my arm, and waited.

Once again, He spoke softly to my heart: *Hear Me at the moment and obey; that's all you have to do. Remember, child, I learned obedience through My suffering.* Then He was gone, leaving me with my thoughts.

After a long time—I don't know how long—bubbles of joy began to form way down deep inside me. They felt so good that I almost forgot about my pain. By using the last of my strength, I managed to turn on my side toward the wall, preparing for sleep. Nurse Curious came in to take my pulse, but I don't think she noticed that my face was damp with tears.

Lord Jesus, it was Your victory today where we walked. Where will You take me tomorrow?

15
The Queen of the Nile

Several days later I was in my little cubicle singing to Jesus, when I heard a festive celebration coming down the hall. What a strange sound for a hospital! I thought I had already heard every type of conversation, every conceivable kind of noise—but this carnival-like commotion was different.

Savoring the break in the monotony of hospital life, I strained my neck and got all prepared for a good look at the intrusion—thankful that my door was open and I had a ringside seat. When the entourage came into view, the sight of it was even more unbelievable than the sound. A contraption resembling an old-fashioned iron bedstead on wheels was being pushed down the hall. On the bed, a most attractive young woman lounged against a mound of pillows. Immediately I thought of Cleopatra, the Queen of the Nile, floating down the river on her barge. The bed was being pushed by an overly attentive young man with whom The Queen was chitchatting like a debutante at a coming-out party. Their voices and laughter almost drowned out the music of the small radio attached to her pink satin pillow. Flowers were hanging all around the bed—some in baskets, some in little straw bowls, some in nosegays.

As this procession vanished from my sight and the hilarity died away in the distance, I wondered if I had really seen it or if I was hallucinating. *This hospital will never be the same,* I thought.

In all the excitement, I had hardly noticed when my lunch tray was brought in—but now I gave it my attention. Although I had no appetite, I tried to drink the coffee and the milk from the little carton. Then I lay back on the pillow, to savor the memory of the drama I had just witnessed.

Get up, Helen. I was surprised by this unexpected command from God.

Yes, Lord. Where are we going?

I want you to go down and meet her.

I knew He meant the Queen of the Nile. *The girl who just went by, Lord? On the float?*

Yes. I want you to go down to see her.

As I inched my legs across the sheet and swung them off the bed, I had a feeling of excitement. I could hardly wait to see what the Lord had in mind.

I began walking down the hall and soon noticed that I was getting into the ward section. At the end of the corridor I turned to the right—and there, dead ahead of me, was the flower-decked bed, jammed into a five-bed ward barely large enough for two beds. The Queen didn't see me.

Lord, what's this all about? He didn't answer, but I knew that, for now, I was just to glimpse where she lay. That was all He wanted me to do.

Two days later, as I was taking my afternoon stroll, the Lord told me to go to The Queen's room again. By this time I was growing stronger, more sure of myself as I walked. I turned my feet toward the ward section—and when I did, the Lord gave me a mental picture of a little rabbit scurrying around through the forest, poking his head here and there into and around the undergrowth. I could see he was terrified.

That is how she feels, the Lord told me. *She is terribly frightened.*

When I went into The Queen's room, she was lying back in bed, watching television. With a shock, I realized that her head was completely bald, covered only by a green shower cap. Without her glamorous wig, she looked like an entirely different person. All the makeup was gone, and with it all the gaiety. I felt that I was seeing the real woman for the first time. One shoulder was in a heavy cast, and her bed—no longer bedecked with flowers—was sitting right out in the middle of the ward. She looked so vulnerable!

I walked over to the bed and introduced myself. Tugging at her plastic shower cap with her one good arm, she responded to my introduction by saying, "Please excuse my looks." I gave her what I hoped was a reassuring smile and was trying to think of a remark to match, when she suddenly burst out with, "I'm frantic!"

I must definitely be the grandmotherly type, I thought. *First Patricia and now The Queen seem to want to bare their souls to me.*

Aloud, I said, "There's no need to be frantic. The Savior is right here beside you, and He's going to keep you in His care."

I surprised myself by using such a direct approach with this stranger, but I felt an immediate positive response from her. She listened to every word, apparently grateful for each hopeful thought as I talked to her about Jesus. "He died on the cross to take away our fears as well as our sins," I told her, "and He has promised never to leave us nor forsake us." (See Hebrews 13:5.) Then I told her about the Comforter, who was His Spirit sent to live in us and walk beside us. I assured this frightened woman that He could bring her into a whole new life, replacing her frantic searching with His peace and joy.

As I was talking to her, I saw God take the fear right out of her heart. The tenseness left her small body, and she sank back onto the pillows. I started to say something else to her, but then I noticed that she was looking beyond me. Turning around, I saw a man standing behind me with a big grin on his face. She introduced him as her surgeon. Surprised at his youthful appearance, I said, "I thought you must be one of her college friends." That seemed to please them both. Recognizing that it was time for me to clear out, I bade her good-bye and promised to pray for her during the day.

The next morning God said, *Helen, go down to see your queenly friend.* I gladly obeyed—but when I arrived at the ward her bed was empty. One of the nurses directed me to a private room two doors away. It was a beautiful room, twice as large as the ward she had left.

When I walked in, she exclaimed, "Oh, Helen, I feel like a princess!" She looked every inch a princess. Her attractive blond wig was back on her head, and she was wearing a beautiful satin gown trimmed with handmade lace. Sitting down by her bed, I smiled at her.

"Would you please pull the covers up over me?" she asked. "I'm cold." Somehow the words came out sounding like a queenly command.

As I spread the blanket over her feet, an orange rolled out from the covers. I smiled and retrieved it for her. Just then, a nurse came in and handed her a carton of milk and some crackers. The Queen explained that she found it comforting to eat in the middle of the night while she watched television. That remark gave me the clue that the peace she had experienced yesterday had been only temporary. I sensed that her whole life was in tumult—but at that time I had no idea *how* tumultuous it was.

After the nurse left and she was all settled down in the bed, she turned huge brown eyes toward me. "I want to talk to you," she said.

Feeling that this "true confession" would be lengthy, I made myself as comfortable as I could in the huge black leather recliner, then smiled at her encouragingly. I wasn't sure I was strong enough to sit there for a long time and listen—but as she began to tell me about her life I soon forgot myself. The story unfolded like a soap opera. Among other things, I learned that she was divorced and had two little daughters. Dissatisfied with her present rather amazing lifestyle, she was trying to decide whether to try to make another life for her children where she now lived or to move with them to another state, where they could live with her wealthy aunt.

I knew God wasn't wasting His time and mine by having me sit there and listen to her sometimes sordid story just for my own amazement. He had a purpose in having her tell me all this, and I was just waiting to find out what it was.

As her plaint went on, I felt my strength draining away. I braced my arm against the recliner and silently asked for help. Occasionally I tried to interrupt the flow of words by introducing Jesus into the conversation—but it was like shadow-boxing. Yesterday, she had appeared to absorb each word I said about Him. Today, whenever I tried to talk about the Savior's power to help her, she would change the subject back to divorce or some other aspect of her problem. I would change it back to Jesus, telling her how He could come into her heart and give her a new life. Then she would say something like, "I don't know whether to move there, to keep the children here, or what."

Seeing that she was hedging, I decided this was not the time to urge her to think seriously about Christ—so I bade her good-bye and went back to my room. I felt totally drained—physically, emotionally, and spiritually.

The next time I went back to visit The Queen, she was asleep. I left my name and telephone number on her bedside table, with a note telling her to call me if she wanted to talk. For the next day or two, I heard nothing from her and made no effort to phone her or see her. Then the Lord said to me, *Go down to your new friend's room.*

Knowing He meant The Queen, I immediately followed instructions. When I got to her room, the door was wide open and the heavy green curtain around her bed was pulled back. There she lay, dressed in the scantiest pair of shorts I have ever seen this side of the beach. Her feet were propped straight up against the wall, and she was chatting on the telephone. Like me, all the people who passed her room were staring at her. She acknowledged me with a little wave of her hand but didn't beckon me to come in. I stood watching her for a moment and then decided it was time for me to bow out of the picture.

As I turned around, I almost laughed at the sight of a young man standing inside the elevator opposite her room. All agog, he was staring at The Queen. When the elevator door began to close, I could see him peering through the crack in order to feast his eyes on the beautiful sight as long as he possibly could.

I was torn between amusement and disgust. Also (I had to be honest with myself) this "good and mighty Christian" was experiencing pangs of jealousy over The Queen's good looks—especially her good-looking legs, since I felt short-changed in that department. As I walked down the hall, I really had a battle with my thoughts.

Lord, I'm torn asunder! What did I do wrong? She was interested in hearing about You at first—or was she just pretending?

Thoughts of love, came the reply.

Think thoughts of love toward her, *Lord? That will take some doing! She was just faking interest—and I sat there using up all my strength while I listened to her self-centered monologue.*

When we mix emotions of jealousy and disgust, we have a lethal combination. I tried to pray for this beautiful, brazen woman, but my prayers were empty. The Lord made it clear that I needed to pray for myself first.

Back in bed, I asked Him to take all the jealousy out of me and help me feel compassion for The Queen. Then the spiritual warfare began. Sitting up in bed, I alternately rebuked Satan and talked to the Lord. Finally, I was able to hear *Him* talking to me.

What is the real reason you're upset? Instantly, in my mind's eye, I saw myself as a little blonde girl on a school playground, surrounded by a group of taunting children. "Cripple, cripple, granny hop," they cried. Then they drew a line around me and trapped me inside a circle they formed by linking arms. My eyes filled with tears at the memory of my childhood sufferings.

At that moment, the Lord spoke to me again, softly, in a voice full of love: *Blessed are the merciful: for they shall obtain mercy* (Matthew 5:7).

No one's ever shown me *any mercy*! was my instant response. Then, to justify my unmerciful attitude toward The Queen, I said, *But, Lord, surely she must know better than to expose her body like that!*

He would not let me change the focus from me. *You are ashamed of your limping and your scars,* He told me. Then I heard Him ask, *How many times, daughter?* His voice was kind.

How many times what *Lord?*

Forgive your sister, Helen, came the reply.

She's not my sister, I snapped.

She will be eventually.

Ashamed, I drew in my breath sharply.

Does her poor taste really matter? I forgave the whole world. Can't you forgive just one person whose behavior offends you?

Then He said something that almost tore my heart in two: *When are you going to forgive* Me, *daughter? You still think I caused you to be physically handicapped. It was not I but our enemy who did this. . . . But have you forgotten what I told you long ago: that I* allowed *it for My glory?* [See John 9:2,3.] *You don't have to understand it. Just* forgive *Me and trust Me to work this and* all *your suffering into a pattern for your good.*

Lord!!! Almost overwhelmed by this revelation, I felt physically sick. I fell back on my pillow and spent the next few hours, between snatches of fitful sleep, pondering what God had just said to me.

Never before had I realized that my subconscious mind was still blaming *God* for the untold physical, mental, and emotional pain created by my childhood bout with osteomyelitis. As the Holy Spirit convicted me of this truth, I sobbed out my confession of guilt and asked His forgiveness.

The afternoon passed in a blur of repentance, tears, gratitude, and thanksgiving. After I forgave God and received His forgiveness, I was able to forgive The Queen and to pray for her with compassion and even love.

When Tuck came to see me after supper, I was a new person, bathed in the light and love of a merciful, gracious, *transforming* God. Seeing that my husband was weary and needed only my love and some small talk, I said nothing to him about The Queen or about the spiritual warfare I had been engaged in that afternoon. But when he left, my mind returned to The Queen. *I can still pray privately for her salvation,* I told myself, *and surely God will answer. I must learn not to be so easily discouraged.*

As I made my bedtime preparations, I gave myself a final pep talk: "Face up to it, kid. Not everybody you witness to is going to pray the sinner's prayer immediately, while you're standing there listening. So you just do your part and trust God to do His."

As I drifted off to sleep, my thoughts of The Queen were thoughts of love.

16

The Swing Shift

The night shift on my hall was a never-failing source of interest to me. The quieted halls sometimes erupted into moments of drama, hinted at by muted sounds, sudden flashes of light, and the scurrying of rubberized footsteps. Sensing the importance of events taking place around me, I practiced praying without ceasing (see 1 Thessalonians 5:17).

Word had apparently gone out that Mother Confessor was in Room 321, and there was a steady stream of traffic through my room after visiting hours were over for the day. Perhaps it was because many patients were sleeping and the staff was less rushed, or perhaps it was because things that lie quiet in the day have a way of going "bump in the night."

Conscious of the opportunity I had to witness to the hospital staff, as well as to my visitors, I kept a little tray of tracts near the fruit basket on the bedside table, handy and ready to share. One night while lying awake, I was surprised to hear light footsteps enter my room and pause at the bedside table. No one spoke. In the light that came from the hall, I could barely make out the outline of my silent visitor's white-uniformed figure; but I watched through one squinted eye as she sifted through the little pile of tracts on the tray. Then, apparently satisfied, Nurse Night-Raider turned sharply and left the room as quietly as she had come in. I didn't know what she had taken, but when Tuck visited me the next day, he proudly announced that someone had thumbtacked a selection of my tracts to the bulletin board in the third-floor waiting room.

"God gets His job done in the most mysterious ways," I commented, before telling Tuck about Nurse Night-Raider. Again I remembered that Paul planted and Apollos watered, but God gave the increase.

One of the night nurses (I soon named her Nurse Nuptials) never failed to come by to see me several times during her shift. At least once every night she took time to tell me about the problems she was having with her fiancé, George, and his friend Ernest.

Ernest and George had bought a big house in an older section of the town and were remodeling it together. The plan was for Ernest to do the carpentry work and George and his fiancée to do the painting and decorating. After their marriage, Nurse Nuptials and George would move into the upstairs apartment and Ernest would live downstairs. According to the nurse, the agreement wasn't working out. Ernest was building kitchen cabinets, closets, and storage spaces, she said, but they were all downstairs in *his* part of the house.

It was easy to tell, from the way she moved things around on my dresser, when Nurse Nuptials and her boyfriend had had an argument. As she became increasingly annoyed with George for not doing anything about the situation at the house, her movements grew more and more abrupt. If something wasn't done about George, I feared I wasn't going to survive the night shifts.

One night I said to her, "Honey, I've got something for you," and I gave her a tract. She took it politely, like a well-trained child trying to please her mother. It was obvious that she had no real interest in it. I began to pray seriously for this young woman.

The next night, when Nurse Nuptials came in to see me, she pulled the bottom sheet so tight that I felt as if I were lying on a trampoline. When she plumped up my pillow, I could almost hear the geese on the lake quacking in sympathy. Finally, she told me she had notified George that he and Ernest could live up on the top floor and she'd stay downstairs with the kitchen cabinets. Not knowing how to settle the argument, I retreated beneath the sheets and asked God to help them.

I was relieved when Nurse Nuptials finally reported to me that she and George had decided to call off their engagement. To me, this seemed the only sensible solution. If a couple begins fighting over closet space *before* the wedding, I figure their marriage is off to a shaky start.

I tried to witness to this troubled young woman as best I could, but I have long since learned that you can't push Jesus on anybody. The Lord has to open a door—and if you're in tune with His Spirit at all times you'll know when that door is open. Until then, it is best to pray and keep silent. This was clearly a time for intercession, not intervention.

The last time Nurse Nuptials came into my room for advice, I simply listened and kept my mouth shut. By deliberately taking my hands off her situation, I was allowing God to work in her life in His own way.

Late one night, I was awakened by the soft glow of a flashlight, held by a nurse I had never seen before. Her kind, mature face reflected past sorrow, but an inner beauty shone from her countenance as she moved quietly around my bed to check the machine and see that all was well with me. My heart was filled with compassion for Nurse Kind-n-Tender, and I longed to get up out of the bed and minister to *her* needs. Although I could only smile weakly and pat her arm, I think she understood. She smiled at me as she picked up her flashlight and turned to go.

After she had left, the suffering reflected in her face lingered in my mind. When the words of a little Scripture song came to me, I softly sang them aloud as my prayer for her:

> He gave me beauty for ashes,
> The oil of joy for mourning,
> The garment of praise for
> The spirit of heaviness.
> (See Isaiah 61:3)

I must have fallen asleep—for how long I don't know—but suddenly I was wide awake and struggling to breathe. Gasping for air, I strained to reach the call bell attached to my pillow. As I turned, fiery pain shot through my shoulder. *Lord, help me*! I groped frantically for the call bell and accidentally pulled on the tubing attached to the bottle of glucose. It flayed wildly around my head, and I feared the whole contraption would come down on top of me.

Fighting for breath, I inched my bandaged shoulder along the pillow, trying to maneuver into a position where I could reach the bell before losing consciousness. As I felt darkness creeping over my brain, I wondered desperately if I would get help in time.

Then I remembered I was not alone in the room. *Don't panic,* I told myself. *Jesus is here. You will be all right.* I stretched one finger toward the bright red button of the call bell. When I felt its smooth surface under my fingertip, I leaned backward, pushing it with all my waning strength.

"Help me! I'm going," I whispered to the voice that answered from the black box at the head of the bed. I wasn't sure *where* I was going, but I knew it would be somewhere in darkness.

Almost instantly, Nurse Kind-N-Tender was there beside me.

"Can't breathe," I gasped. "Don't let me faint." As I said those words, the darkness closed in around me.

From somewhere far in the distance, I could hear the sound of rubber-soled shoes running on tile floors. *Where could they be going?* The darkness was intense. I tried to remember where I was. Opening my eyes cautiously, I saw three white-uniformed figures moving about my bed. *Lord, I'm so cold*!

Something damp and cool lay on my neck—a cloth. It felt good, but it didn't warm me up. Where was my sheet? A soft light now shone full in my face. Nurse Kind-N-Tender was standing by my bed, holding my hand.

"We're going to give you a shot," she said. "It will help you rest." In a soft, firm voice, she gave directions to the other nurses who were working over me.

Lord, what are they doing? I felt drowsy and nauseated at the same time.

"I feel sick."

"It will soon pass," was the reply.

Once again, darkness overtook me.

The next morning, I slept through Dr. Strong-Flower's early visit. Throughout the day, dreams drifted in and out of my mind, bringing disturbing thoughts from my subconscious. I must have been having one of those dreams when the doctor came in for his evening rounds, because I was shaking wildly and mumbling in my sleep. Placing his hand on my foot—almost the only part of me that wasn't bandaged or hooked up to tubes—he shook me gently, calling my name.

As I opened my eyes, they focused on a man's coat sleeve. *That's strange,* I thought. Gradually I became aware of a row of silver buttons on a navy blazer, then of gray slacks and polished black shoes. These were all I could see without moving my head—and that required too much effort. Forcing myself back to full consciousness, I finally moved my eyes slowly upward until I recognized Dr. Strong-Flower standing there beside my bed. I had never seen him before without his starched white coat. He seemed different somehow.

"Are you going to a party?" I asked him weakly. Then I paused. *Lord, have I been too personal?* My brain felt dull, unresponsive.

Although he didn't answer my question, Dr. Strong-Flower's tone reassured me as he asked, "What happened to you last night, young lady?" I smiled at his charitable description of me, recognizing that it was part of his professional bedside manner.

"I have my version," Dr. Strong-Flower continued, "but I want yours too."

"Well, I just fainted, I guess. I've never had an experience like that before . . . things went black, and I couldn't get my breath . . . I felt faint . . . sick . . ."

"How do you feel now?" he questioned.

"I can't describe how I feel. I've just had a terrible dream."

He moved nearer to my bed, chuckling quietly. "My son has an old 'Sooner' dog," he said. " 'Sooner be one breed as another.' She lies on the hearth and shakes in her sleep every night. Not that I'm comparing you with old Sooner. But when I came in here, you were moaning and shaking in your sleep just like she does when she's lying by the fire and it gets too hot. I think she dreams about chasing rabbits. What were *you* dreaming about?"

His voice was kind as he joked with me, but I knew him well enough to realize he was serious. Whatever had brought on the attack the previous night had caused him concern, and he meant to get to the bottom of it. Although I couldn't help him find the cause, I was well aware that the death angel had paid a midnight call—but my heavenly Father had met him at the door.

As Dr. Strong-Flower reached for the metal chart case hanging at the foot of my bed, I was writing with my imagination across last night's entries in bold letters: "THERE IS NO POWER BUT OF GOD! [Romans 13:1] HALLELUJAH!!"

17

The Medicine of a Merry Heart

Before I entered the hospital, I determined to do two things to help the people who loved me or cared for my welfare: First, I would not complain; second, I would be cheerful and cooperative. I wished my mother could know that the wonderful training she gave me as a child was bearing fruit in my attitude toward "life's rough spots," as she called calamities. Complaining was foreign to Mother's nature; so was self-pity. God had blessed her with a gift of spontaneous laughter that filled our house with merriment and still rings in my memory. (I can hear her voice now, echoing through my childhood—joking, bantering, clowning with her children. She seemed to be forever young.) How thankful I am that I inherited the saving gift of laughter from her!

Among the greatest blessings the Father has bestowed on the human race, I am convinced, is a sense of humor. All my life, the ability to sense and enjoy the comical, even the ridiculous, has helped me through many a trying situation. It stood me in good stead during my hospital stay.

Since I couldn't remain in an attitude of prayer and meditation during *all* my waking hours, I learned to brighten the days by watching the daily goings-on in the hall outside my door. I was alert to the doctors, nurses, patients, and visitors who passed by—in fact, to everything that came within the range of my five senses. Sometimes a hearty laugh in the hall, without any visual contact, would trigger spontaneous laughter from me. Sometimes there were pathos and tears—reminders to pray for others as well as myself. After a while, I began to recognize the footsteps of several individuals who frequented the hall. I learned to distinguish many of the doctors and some of the nurses by the way they walked—but I never could recognize Dr. Strong-Flower's walk. He always came so quietly that the first thing I heard was his perfunctory bang on the swinging door to my room. I guess he thought he was giving me time to hide my modesty under the bedsheet. Why did he bother? I was already swathed like an Egyptian mummy. Nevertheless, I appreciated my doctor's warning knock. It gave me time to clear my throat and get ready to answer his questions.

With more practice, I even learned exactly how many steps a habitual visitor would take before hesitating, then knocking and entering a certain door. After the knock, I would try to anticipate the first words usually spoken by that visitor, and say them aloud: "How's it coming today?" or "You're looking good," or "Howdy, howdy!" A childish game, to be sure—but it helped pass some lagging moments.

Another childish game that helped keep my sense of humor working was that of giving secret nicknames to the members of the staff—Nurse Needlepoint, for example. I'll never forget the first day she came into my room to do her duty. A huge hypodermic needle in her right hand, she hit my door with the palm of her left hand. The noise exploded the quietness of my room. Believe me, I came fully awake!

"Stick 'em up!" she demanded—or at least, that's the way I interpreted her order to go through my arm-raising exercise. I dared not disobey such an authoritative command—so my arm began its torturous journey through the air, stopping midway.

"Higher! Reach for the ceiling!"

I felt like an actress in an old-fashioned cowboy movie. Even though I was the victim of this "hold-up," the humor of the scene did not escape me. As my arm reached back into its over-the-head routine, a pain resembling white heat shot up my arm and back down into my shoulder blade. I winced, but kept my mouth shut. I was scared to say anything. Better to suffer in silence than to disobey Nurse Needlepoint.

"That's better," she said. "Now move over."

I gritted my teeth and, with all my strength, ground one leg into the bed, putting all my weight on the opposite side. Then I thrust the other leg across, and I was over! At least she couldn't shoot me for disobedience.

Impassionately, with one long sweep of her arm, Nurse Needlepoint yanked the overhead lamp down, spotlighting my bed within the circle of its bright yellow beam. I shivered and tried to shrink down under the covers. Out of the corner of one eye, I was horrified to spot a flash of steel descending toward my shaking body. As her hypodermic weapon came closer, I squinted my eyes tight shut and held my breath, every muscle taut, body quivering in anticipation of pain. After what seemed an eternity, my eyes popped open just in time to see the needle come down with a giant thrust and enter the soft, fleshy tubing of the glucose bottle. When I finally realized that Nurse Needlepoint had emptied the contents of her syringe into the glucose bottle instead of my arm, my sigh of relief sounded like air escaping from an overinflated balloon.

Without another word, Nurse Needlepoint turned and stalked triumphantly out of the room, leaving the door swinging on its hinges. The shoot-out was over, and we had both won!

Limp with relief, I lay in bed and gave free rein to the memories evoked by Nurse Needlepoint's performance. Almost every Saturday of my childhood, my sisters and I spent a dime apiece to see the cowboy matinee at the local movie theater. The actors and actresses strutted around in their fancy hats and cowboy boots, looking as if they owned the ranch. They sauntered in and out of scenes, rarely changing their expressions. Even as a child, I would laugh at the way the cowboys stood wooden-faced and tongue-tied, stealing side glances at the ladies, then suddenly whirling around to pat their horses and kiss *them* on the neck. Even though it all seemed ridiculous to me, my sisters and I would sit through two or three showings of the same movie, chewing on our Black Cow suckers as we cheerfully waited for the reel to be rewound in the projection box. Mom would come looking for us (I don't know how she found us in the dark, but she always did) and would drag us home, asking why in the world we stayed so long looking at the same show over and over. When we came out of the theater, we were always surprised that it was almost dark; it seemed such a short time since we had gone in right after lunch.

One comical highlight of my hospital stay was inadvertently provided by Friend Helen. On one of her visits, she went into the dark cave of my antiquated bathroom to wash some gowns for me. Seeing a cord hanging from the ceiling, she gave it a yank—but the bathroom remained dark.

"How do you turn on the light in here?" she asked, coming back into the room with my nightgowns draped all over her arms. Just then, three wild-eyed nurses burst through my swinging door and raced into the room. Startled out of our wits, Helen and I just stared at them.

"What's the matter?" one of them demanded, as they stood like three white-starched statues in a grouping titled "Controlled Panic."

Having no idea what they were talking about, Helen and I remained mute, though Helen did manage to shake her head. The sight of my nightgowns hanging on Helen's arm gave The Rescue Squad the clue to what had happened, and their anxiety turned to a mixture of amusement and annoyance. It seems that the cord Helen had innocently pulled had triggered an emergency alarm at the nurses' station, and that in turn had triggered their mad dash to my room.

Helen and I both apologized profusely—but after the nurses left, Helen began snickering. I soon joined in, and before long we were laughing uproariously. I finally had to get Helen to lower the head of my bed and terminate her visit, leaving my gowns unwashed. I was worn out by the exertion and excitement—the most I had had since my surgery—but the laughter was like medicine to my bones (see Proverbs 17:22). I was immensely grateful to learn that my sense of humor was still intact, and that I was still tapped into Solomon's wise counsel: One of the conditions of good health is a glad and happy mind.

Determined to be glad and happy, regardless, I was soon aware that all of the little dramas of life enacted around my bed could help promote my health and welfare and that of my family. So I joked with all the jokable, rejoiced with the rejoicing, and laughed with the merry in heart.

There was one little nurse's aide who seemed to enjoy laughter as much as I did. One morning she bounced into my room, hands behind her back, and a whopping grin on her ruddy Irish face.

"Got somethin' for ya this mornin'! Guess what it is!"

She had captured my immediate interest.

"What is it, Irish, a time bomb?"

"Better'n that!" she joshed back. "It's somethin' you've been lyin' awake dreamin' about, you want it so bad."

With a wide, dramatic sweep of her arm, she placed a gaily wrapped package at the foot of my bed, just out of my reach.

"Guess," she urged me again.

"Can't imagine."

With that, she whipped open the wrappings, and out fell a blue enameled sliver of a bedpan.

"Now you won't have to wait for us any more," she chortled. "From now on, you've got full permission to get out of this bed and walk around this hospital any time you want. This is just a reminder that once you were bound and now you are free."

We laughed and laughed, anticipating together the enjoyment of my new privileges. That night, the nurse was pleasantly surprised at how well I ate my supper. After she had picked up my tray, I heard her announce to the hall outside my room, "Mrs. Tucker's got her appetite back." The joking little aide had produced medicine they could not have administered with a needle.

When I had been too ill to read, watch TV, or listen to music, I had spent most of the hours in quietness, except for an occasional visit from some thoughtful minister who found my name in the file downstairs. During my entire hospital stay, a total of fifteen ministers visited my little quarters to bless me. I was immensely grateful.

When Dr. Strong-Flower had restricted visitors and telephone calls, I was often thrown into the private world of my thoughts. The lone intrusion of white-clad figures brought only momentary respite as they floated in and out of the drama enacted on the stage of my mind. They took their places unknowingly, acted out their respective parts, spoke their lines, and exited my stage.

The nurses who came into my room on routine business at all hours of the day and night varied in shape, size, voice, personality, and appearance—and each had a different role to play in the hospital drama. One of the most interesting members of the *dramatis personae* was Nurse Kok-a-Doo, who played the same role in the same scene at the same time each day.

Bright and early each morning, she would strut into my room and crow, "Goodmorning,/Mrs./Tucker. It's/almost/seven/(sing-song)o'clock. Get/up/and/take/your/bath/and/get/ready/for/breakfast." All her words ran together like water drops down a drainpipe. Then she'd go into the bathroom and ceremoniously lay out on my sink a thin washcloth saturated with cold water. After that, she would stand at the door with one hand on her hip, preening her black feathery hair, until she saw some sign of life under the sheets. Satisfied with any movement from the bed, she turned dramatically, then strutted out just as cockily as she had come in.

Sometimes I thought there *must* be a better way for the day to begin—even in a hospital. The morning finally came, however, when I had no trouble whatsoever responding to Nurse Kok-a-Doo's call.

18

"Victory Day"

On one very special Saturday morning, I awoke with a sense of excitement and an awareness that this was the long-awaited, promised Victory Day. As I was wiping my face with the icy washcloth prepared for me by Nurse Kok-a-Doo, I thought about what Dr. Strong-Flower had told me yesterday, when he promised I could go *home* today! He said he was well pleased with the way my body was responding to treatment—and he was leaving orders for me to be discharged the next day (Saturday), even though he himself would be out of town for the weekend. I myself had begun to feel renewed strength—and in spite of the fact that I had waked up with a scratchy throat, I felt stronger than ever on this long-awaited day of my release.

With a deep sense of gratitude, I whispered, "Praise You, Jesus! This is the day that the Lord hath made. I will rejoice and be glad in it." (See Psalm 118:24.) I began singing those words under my breath, but before I knew it I was singing aloud: "This is the day, this is the day . . ."

When Miss Gourmet came in with my breakfast tray, she was delighted to discover that my appreciation for her food offerings had greatly increased since the day before. For the first time, I accepted the tray with enthusiasm. Wrapping the sheet around me, toga fashion, I dangled my legs over the side of the bed, then jerked off the silver cover as though I really meant business. On my plate lay scrambled eggs and three slices of bacon. A cup of steaming coffee gave off a tempting aroma. The tray also held a bowl of cold Cream of Wheat, covered with a heavy crust. I quickly plopped the silver cover over it to hide its pathetic state; no need to ruin my appetite before I had tasted my food. Surprisingly enough, I felt famished—and some hot food would feel good to my sore throat.

I snapped the crispy bacon between my front teeth and was in the process of enjoying my eggs when I was startled by the sound of a heavy hand striking my swinging door. I made a grab for the sheet, in an effort to cover myself more effectively, just as a white pantsuit appeared in the doorway. It belonged to a nurse I had never seen before, but she immediately acquired the name "Nurse Pugilist."

"Put your food away," she commanded. "The doctor wants to see you." Her attractive face was expressionless, her voice commanding, her manner almost threatening. Gingerly easing my over-the-bed table to one side and pulling my legs back into bed, I mentally told my breakfast good-bye. *Strange that I don't get to eat the first time I've really been hungry,* I thought vaguely. I wondered if I should call the dietitian for counsel. She had so longed to see the day when I would finally learn to appreciate her culinary delights.

No sooner had I tucked my protesting body under the sheet than I heard an even louder thud—in no way resembling a knock—against my door. It was followed immediately by the entrance of a large man I had never seen before. *Dr. Hammerhead will be his name,* I thought, observing his mode of entering the room. He wore casual but expensive sport clothes: a navy cashmere cardigan, grey flannel slacks sans belt, and loafer-type shoes with small black tassels that bounced as he walked. From his manner and dress, I suspected he was on the golf-playing circuit. Giving me a quick glance, he walked over to the foot of my bed and picked up my chart. After glancing at it briefly, he closed the cover with a sharp clap of metal and took a tongue depressor from Nurse Pugilist. By squeezing his robust middle between the bed and the wall, he managed to get close enough to me to inspect my throat.

"You're not to go home today," he announced flatly, avoiding eye contact with me. While I was digesting that unsettling bit of information, he continued, "Got anybody there to look after you?"

Stammering a bit, I said, "Well, my husband—"

"Won't do. Don't you know you're too d___ weak to leave here? What if you fainted or something when you're all alone?"

I was too shocked and disheartened to put up a protest. Dr. Hammerhead walked toward the door, proclaiming over his shoulder just before he exited, "Only a fool would play golf in weather like this." Even in my disappointment, I mentally congratulated myself for having guessed he was a golfing enthusiast.

Nurse Pugilist turned on her rubber heels and followed Dr. Hammerhead out of the room. Something about their actions suggested finality. Reeling from this disconcerting development, I collapsed under the security of the covers to contemplate my changed prospects and try to come to terms with them. My once-tempting breakfast, now cold and neglected, no longer held any appeal.

Lord, what's it all about?

The answer came swiftly: *The trial of your faith.*

Dr. Hammerhead had been gone only a few minutes when the door banged open again and in came Nurse Pugilist, the undisputed featherweight champion of the east wing. From the way her lower lip was curled, I could tell she still had on her mental boxing gloves. Having accepted—albeit unwillingly—Dr. Hammerhead's verdict that I remain incarcerated in the hospital for an indefinite stay, I felt that I was already kayoed and lying out cold on the canvas. Even an amateur like me, however, could sense that the old champion was spoiling for another fight.

Being a natural-born coward, I quickly grabbed up my white sheet and frantically waved the corner of it in the air as a flag of truce. She didn't even see it; she just kept advancing toward my bed with a glint in her eye that I hadn't noticed before.

I resorted to another cowardly maneuver. "I don't feel so good," I whimpered.

Nurse Pugilist paid no attention to this plea for sympathy. "Did you hear what he said?" she demanded, looking down at me from the exalted position of champion.

"Yes, I heard what—" I began.

"He said you got no business leaving the hospital; you're too weak."

"Yes, ma'am," I whispered in a barely audible voice.

"Did you hear what else he said? He said, 'You get back in that bed; you stay right there; you are not to be released today.' "

Instant replay, I thought—but out loud I said only, "Yes, ma'am. That's all right."

"Then why are you crying?"

"I don't know," I replied. "I guess I'm just weak."

"Why are you weak?" Before I could answer, she repeated the question: "*Why are you weak?*"

"I don't know" I said again.

Triumphant, she answered her own question. "You're too sick to be let out of this hospital—that's why!"

There it was—my second kayo! Sniffling a bit, I slid further down in bed and pulled the covers up to my nose to indicate that I accepted defeat. After looking at me unsympathetically for a few seconds, Nurse Pugilist took her hands off her hips and, turning smugly on her heel, strutted out—clearly the winner.

I didn't know why she had come to my turf for a return match. Had I put up a fight, or even presented a challenge to Dr. Hammerhead concerning my discharge from the hospital? I didn't think so.

As I sank further into what I hoped would be oblivion, my spiritual eyes were suddenly opened and a tremendous thought occurred to me: These people had only my best interests at heart. They were protecting my health! I lay quietly, meditating on this insight.

From my memory came the words of a favorite verse of Scripture, put to music: "Therefore with joy shall ye draw water out of the wells of salvation" (Isaiah 12:3). I forced myself to hum the tune aloud, feeling in my spirit that something important was to follow.

Then I heard my Father speak to me: *Child, you've got the well of salvation down in your innermost being. Haven't I said that would be so? When you accepted My Son Jesus as your Savior, His Spirit was formed in you. So now I say, you are to go down inside yourself and to draw joy from the well of salvation. Meditate on My Word.*

As I considered what the Father had said, I had to confess that I still wasn't in any mood to rejoice in my salvation. My whole constitution had been momentarily shaken by Nurse Pugilist's verbal attack, and I had decided to have a little sympathy-for-self session right there in my bed. Maybe I could even pout a little. But God was telling me now to draw *joy* out of the well of salvation that was in me.

Lord, how am I going to do that in the mood I'm in?

Then came the verse: "*Behold, God is my salvation; I will trust, and not be afraid: for the Lord Jehovah is my strength and my song; he also is become my salvation*" (Isaiah 12:2).

So the *joy* of the Lord was my strength (Nehemiah 8:10), and the *joy* of the Lord was my song, and the *joy* of the Lord had become my salvation! Slowly the joy began to arise from within me. Suddenly, I laughed aloud. The sound echoed through the small confines of my white cubicle, bouncing from wall to wall. It felt so good that I did it again. Why should I let a belligerent nurse intimidate me? *Lord Jesus, I praise Your name! I will sing a new song, for You have done excellent things. I praise You, O Lord, my God!*

My joy soared; my cup of laughter ran over. It no longer mattered whether I was ready to go home and be with my husband. It didn't matter *how* long I had to stay in the hospital. It didn't matter that I was weak. It didn't matter that the nurse had talked to me sharply for no apparent reason. None of these things was of any real consequence.

Another verse came to my mind: "I have learned, in whatsoever state I am, therewith to be content" (Philippians 4:11). If Paul the Apostle could be content in prison with the vermin crawling over him, I could certainly be content in the comfort and security of this hospital.

Many times in the past, God had said to me, *Out of your being shall come rivers of living water* [see John 7:38] *to refresh you, to lift you up, to give you strength*—and I knew "strength" meant whatever I had need of at a particular moment. The Holy Spirit of God Himself lives in my innermost being. *Praise the Lord for such a masterful plan! Praise the Lord for Nurse Pugilist! Bless her especially, Father.*

Jesus understands human nature. He understands all about me, and He wants me to be filled with joy. He knew I would feel intimidated by Nurse Pugilist, and He didn't want me to let anyone or anything ruffle my feathers or take away my joy. That's why He showed me that the resources to conquer *every*thing had to come from down within me—because He, Jesus Christ, is within me! He was telling me to draw from His own inexhaustible supply of strength, peace, and joy.

Right there in Room 321, I made a new resolve to practice in a *real* way all the things He had been trying to teach me over the past years—all the lessons and all the Scriptures He had been putting in my heart. *Now* was the time to see how they truly work. I reminded myself that the power of God is *within* me—not something I receive from an external source. I had fallen into a habit of praying, "Please send me Your peace. Please give me Your love." No longer! The inner woman—*me*—*contains* the Spirit of God, who *is* all these things. I am "complete in Him" (see Colossians 2:10); in Him I "live, and move, and have [my] being" (Acts 17:28).

Lord, You operate through my body to bring forth what You require of me; for it's Your life within me, Jesus, that brings the fulfillment of all Your promises. What a Savior! What a plan!

This same principle, I saw, was at work to bring forth the healing of my body. When I'm wounded, I heal from within. When I'm sad, the tears of relief come from within. When I'm joyful, the laughter comes from within. At last I was beginning to grasp the magnificent truth that everything I need to be victorious over my circumstances is carried around in my physical body moment by moment, day by day. My needs are continually supplied by the power of Jesus Christ, complete and whole and perfect within me. Everything needed for my spiritual and emotional well-being comes from within me, where Jesus dwells. *Praise be to God!* Happy tears, rich with promise, flowed down my cheeks.

Filled with joy and fresh strength, I prayed aloud, "I determine in my heart, I set my will before God right this minute, to be victorious over this mastectomy. When I get out of the hospital, Lord, I *will* conquer this latest disability. I will live life freely, my spirit unencumbered by my circumstances, You alone being my strength. Amen."

As God's truth continued to come home to me, the victorious words of Saint Paul took on new meaning: "I live; yet not I, but Christ liveth in me" (Galatians 2:20). The Master's strength within me was pitting itself against the bodily weakness produced by this latest physical handicap. I could call on that strength when the pull of gravity against my unbalanced body became overwhelming, as it sometimes did. When my weakness threatened to defeat me, I could be victorious by remembering to offer "thanks . . . to God, which giveth us the victory through our Lord Jesus Christ" (1 Corinthians 15:57).

Dr. Strong-Flower had told me that some women say, after a radical mastectomy, that their bodies feel as if they were "enclosed in an iron vest." I understood now what they meant, for there had been—and would continue to be—times when my body cried out,

"I'm immovable! I'm rigid on one side! My nerve endings are dead! I won't be of any further use to you; I'll just be a stiff iron corset forever."

I decided then and there to refuse such threats—never, never to accept immobility. I would exercise by swimming, Aquacise, walking, and regular workouts at the YWCA. I would do anything and everything that would help keep me agile and "moving" the rest of my life. If times of weakness came—and I knew they would—I must refuse to allow my physical feelings to overcome my faith. Instead, I would take charge of my body by declaring to it: *It's not so! The Lord Jesus Christ is making you new and supple. He is healing the nerve endings, bringing new life. Every part of you, body, is receiving His help from within me. Body, in the name of Jesus Christ my Lord, be filled with new energy, new health, new healing; become a normal, workable body!*

I didn't know it then, but this practice of giving my body its "marching orders" would become as natural as breathing—a whole new way of life. After giving my body its orders, I talk to my Lord: *Jesus, You are making me 100 percent whole, and I shall see it manifested. Thank You, Lord!*

That day in Room 321, I still appeared to be 80 percent helpless—but I knew that Jesus inside me was already 100 percent victorious, and the result was bound to become apparent in many new ways very soon. It was difficult to wait for my healing and for my release from the hospital, but I realized that almighty God created time and knows how to use it for His children's highest good. "My times are in [His] hand" (see Psalm 31:15); I could trust Him.

A final Scripture that came to mind was from 1 Corinthians 10:13: "God is faithful, who will not suffer you to be tempted above that ye are able; but will with the temptation also make a way to escape, that ye may be able to bear it."

At that time, I had no idea how much I would need that promise to sustain me in the days that lay ahead.

19
Going Home

Early the next morning, I woke up and began planning my day in contentment. Although my throat seemed very sore, I had the desire to dress up for my husband's Sunday-morning visit by putting on my prettiest flowered nightgown and robe. After taking a sponge bath, I donned my one exquisite gown, made of a material resembling spun silk. It was so light, so airy, that I could hold it on one finger. I sprayed my most romantic perfume all over me—even on my bandages, hoping it wouldn't soak through. Friends Frances and Dot had supplied me with a tantalizing basketful of beauty products; I sampled them all.

After I had done everything I could to make myself attractive, I lay back in bed—exhausted from the effort, but satisfied. At that moment Nurse Pugilist walked in.

Sniffing the sweet-scented air like a well-trained bloodhound, she said, "Doctor wants to come in to see you." If she noticed the improvement in my appearance since her visits the day before, she failed to comment.

Hardly had she finished her announcement when Dr. Hammerhead strode briskly into the room. With only a nod of greeting, he took out a tongue depressor and told me to open my mouth. After inspecting my throat, he announced to the room that it was very red. Then, muttering something else out of one side of his mouth, he turned around and walked out, Nurse Pugilist close on his heels. I had no idea what he had said to me.

Two seconds later, the nurse came back in—apparently in a great hurry. "Did you hear what he said?" she demanded. A bit startled by the whole episode, I shook my head.

"Did you hear what he said?" she repeated, impatience in her tone and her expression. Vaguely I thought, *Well, this sounds familiar. Seems to me I've heard that somewhere before.*

"No," I answered.

"He said you're dismissed!"

"*Dismissed*?" I asked in astonishment. My face must have revealed my doubts.

"Yes," she replied, "you're dismissed. The papers have already been made out."

Stunned, I remained silent. Whipping out the thermometer on my bedside table, Nurse Pugilist stuck it in my mouth without a word. As she waited for my temperature to register, she reached over and thumbed through a book lying on the table. It was the story of a happily married couple whose lives were made complete in Jesus. Her face as she read registered a mixture of sadness and yearning. The Lord spoke to me very softly: *She has a wretched marriage.* Suddenly, my heart melted with compassion for her, and I closed my eyes to hide the tears.

Lord Jesus, I do pray that You will give me a compassionate, understanding heart. Teach me to listen to what the Spirit is saying. If only I could hear the Spirit before I judge the person I have to do with—O Lord, how different my attitude would be! Lord, I ask to see with Your eyes and hear with Your understanding and love. Help me.

"Your temperature is over 102," Nurse Pugilist informed me. "You're still dismissed, however, and the papers are at the desk." With that, she left.

I immediately telephoned my husband. "Tuck," I wailed, "I've now been dismissed, and I don't know what to do. I feel so out of it."

Tuck was astounded, but he promised to come for me as soon as he could.

As I hung up the phone, I realized I was beginning to feel wretched in my spirit and in my body—completely out of tune with the Spirit of God. I knew Satan was attacking me physically and spiritually. I also knew that the One who lives in me (Jesus) is greater than "he that is in the world" (Satan); but for the moment I failed to appropriate that promise from 1 John 4:4.

Reluctantly and painfully, I climbed out of bed and reached in the closet for the brown pantsuit I had worn to the hospital. I expected someone on the staff to come in and help me pack my bags, but not a soul darkened my door. As I began the almost-forgotten routine of dressing myself, I was thinking, *Those sure must have been powerful cosmetics, to transform me overnight from "too weak to leave the hospital" to "case dismissed."*

By the time Tuck arrived, I was dressed and had packed my clothes in the little plaid suitcase. Gathering up my cards and letters, we tried in vain to get them all in the duffel bag Tuck had brought from home. By the time he had obtained a box from one of the nurses on the floor and we had stuffed the remainder of my cards in that, I was feeling so weak and sick that Tuck had to finish getting my belongings together.

I began to have a feeling of unreality. It was as though the nurses and aides had vanished from the floor and we were there alone. How inconceivable that Those People could pitch me out into the snow, when they knew how sick I was! Tuck's theory was that Dr. Hammerhead had reversed his decision because he became uneasy about defying Dr. Strong-Flower's instructions that I be discharged on Saturday. But Dr. Strong-Flower hadn't known that I would come down with . . .

After Tuck had gone to the office to pay my bill, I went over to the dresser to check the drawers. Then I did something so uncharacteristic that I startled myself. I pulled the drawers open one by one, then loudly banged them shut. The noise reverberated throughout the room, and I hoped it traveled all the way to the nurses' station. After that, I lay down to wait for my husband and talk to my Father.

Lord, what is this all about? My question concerned my own behavior as much as the circumstances of my discharge.

The Father began to talk to me in the gentlest way, showing me that I had banged the drawers shut because I was angry inside—angry and deeply humiliated, my ego crushed. When the Lord showed me what my "insides" looked like, I was ashamed, particularly when I remembered my secret self-congratulation on being so patient, sweet, and loving throughout the whole ordeal. God showed me that, even when I was perfectly controlled on the outside, all of my piety showing itself in the most pleasant ways, inside I was sometimes harboring resentment. It wasn't a pretty picture.

I was still arguing with God when Nurse Serious came in, thermometer in hand. She peeked into my throat, then took my temperature again—even though less than an hour had passed since Nurse Pugilist had taken it. As I sat on the edge of the bed with the thermometer sticking out of my mouth, two great tears started down my cheeks. I knew I was feeling sorry for myself, and that made me feel even *sorrier* for myself. The nurse quickly took the thermometer out of my mouth and asked with concern, "What's the matter?"

"I'm tired, I guess. I'm just tired."

Her expression showed compassion, and I could sense her empathy as she put the thermometer back in my mouth and took my pulse. Silently she recorded her findings on my chart, then turned and left the room.

In a few minutes my husband came back, followed shortly by a nurse's aide with a pushcart. Since Tuck hadn't called her, I knew the staff had been monitoring our progress. Without a word, Nurse's Aide began stacking my luggage, get-well cards, and potted plants on the cart.

"Got everything out of the closet?" Before she was through asking, she had peeked into the closet to check for herself. She seemed to be trying to make amends for the neglect of the other staff members. "Wait a minute," she continued. "I want to get a wheelchair for you."

"Oh, no—nonsense!" I protested, waving my tissues, and fighting against self-pity.

Wisely, Tuck intervened: "No, Helen. Wait."

I knew I was too weak to walk to the car, but I was determined to be a martyr. Puzzled about Dr. Hammerhead's change of mind, and hurt and angry over what I felt was shameful neglect on the part of the staff, I was sick at heart and sick in body.

When Nurse's Aide returned with a wheelchair, she and Tuck carefully put my camel's hair coat around me and helped me get seated. Shaking from the effort, I was grateful for Tuck's steadying arm.

I secretly hoped Nurse Pugilist would be around when we passed the nurses' station: I would smile at her weakly, and she would see how pitiable my condition was and what an awful thing they were doing to me. Nurse Pugilist was nowhere in sight, however, and none of the nurses seemed to be paying any attention to us. Not a soul waved good-bye when Nurse's Aide rolled my wheelchair into the elevator.

When we got to the hospital entrance, I looked at Nurse's Aide and said to my husband, "She's been so good to me. I don't know what in the world I would have done without her." Thereupon, Tuck gave her ten dollars. My unworthy thought was, *Well, I didn't mean that she had given me* that *much love and attention*!

Accepting the money gratefully, Nurse's Aide said, "Will you please pray for me? My elderly mother lives with me, and it's really hard coming to work every morning and leaving her alone." Immediately my conscience stung me for begrudging her the ten-dollar tip. Tears brimmed over, flowing unchecked.

Tuck brought the car up to the door, and he and Nurse's Aide eased me into the front seat. As we drove off, I leaned back against the headrest and dissolved into tears. I was supposed to be a Christian, but I was nothing but a humiliated, angry, self-centered mess. *Now I've blown it,* I thought. *O Lord, how long maturity?*

The sound of snow crunching beneath the tires as we made our way out of the hospital grounds brought me to the sudden realization that I was actually going *home*! How could I ever have thought I wanted to spend more time in the hospital? As Tuck skillfully guided the car over the snow-covered streets, I relaxed beside him and tried to put the memory of the past thirteen days out of my mind. I was grateful to be leaving Room 321 and all it stood for.

My heartbeat accelerated with anticipation as we entered our beloved subdivision. Sprawled out across the land in a coat of crystal and white, the gently rolling hills and slopes sparkled in the light. A Grandma Moses' brush had stroked our beautiful Bellevue Terrace.

Tuck turned the car down our short street, and soon we were climbing the steep, freshly cleared driveway leading into our carport. For one shining moment, I forgot my sore throat and feverish, aching body. At last, I was home again!

20
Stormy Weather

My house had never looked so inviting. As I glanced around at the familiar surroundings, I saw that Prayer Group had spiffed it clean and put flowers everywhere, even on the refrigerator. The kitchen counters were loaded with scrumptious-looking foods of all sorts. I recognized the culinary delights of my friends Helen S. and Libbie. Love's evidences brought swift tears. Oh, it was *good* to be home again!

After getting me settled on the couch in the family room, smothering-warm under a mound of blankets, Tuck announced that he would prepare lunch. Soon I heard him in the kitchen (unfamiliar territory for him) opening cabinets, banging drawers, and poking into tin cans with a metal spoon—probably sterling. I wanted to lend him a hand for self-survival, but he had given me strict orders not to move. From the vantage point of the sofa, I rolled my eyes in his direction, watching him move about the kitchen. The counter tops were loaded with potential disaster traps. The refrigerator door stood wide open; the stove burners glowed red. *Dear Lord, can I live through the trauma of being at home?*

Finally Tuck came back into the family room, triumphantly bearing a brass gallery tray with the results of his efforts. In a plastic bowl was something he called tomato soup: crimson lumps swimming around in lukewarm swirls of pink liquid. Beside the bowl was a five-inch stack of graham crackers. I glanced the other way as he set the tray down in front of me, hoping he wouldn't notice my reaction.

Somehow I didn't have much appetite for the tepid soup, but drinking my milk from the frosty silver goblet was a delight. It went down well with the dill pickle alongside. Tuck had tried hard to please, and I loved him for it.

Later in the afternoon, Tuck left to pick up some essential supplies at the drugstore. His car had hardly backed down the drive when it began snowing again—*hard.* When I turned on my little portable radio to check the weather bulletins, phrases like "power failures," "impassable roads," "record snowfall" did nothing to bring me peace of mind. Would Tuck be able to get home safely?

I was too exhausted to worry long. Turning off the radio, I lay still for a while and soon dropped into a feverish sleep.

It seemed dark everywhere when the sound of Tuck's key in the side door awakened me. Refreshed by my nap, I eagerly waited to welcome him home. He was barely visible in the gathering dusk as he walked into the room and dumped his purchases into the nearest chair.

Instead of a loving greeting, his first words were, "The power is off, Helen! We don't have any heat, and the woodpile outside is frozen." His attorney-voice had taken over. It has a special authoritative edge to it that always comes when he's deeply concerned about something. "I'm going outside to see if the wood on the porch is dry enough to burn in the fireplace." With that he disappeared, banging the door behind him.

Tuck didn't say hello, I thought. *No kiss or anything. He knows my throat is sore and my temperature needs taking, but he didn't even ask how I feel.* Choking back the complaints, I lay sullenly in my cocoon of blankets and concentrated on my hurt feelings. It was easy to brush aside the knowledge that Tuck's single-minded concern for his patient's physical welfare was responsible for his apparent indifference to his wife's emotional needs.

Can't he see that I'm lonely and want to talk? It seems like I've been by myself for hours. Such self-centered thoughts were swirling around in my mind when I heard the side door slam. Tuck came back inside, carrying an armful of wood. He was covered with snow and shivering. After wiping his wet shoes on the carpet just inside the door, he dropped his load in the woodbox by the hearth.

"There's not enough dry wood," he reported. "If the power stays off all night, we're in trouble." His face reflected deep concern. (Although I didn't know it, Dr. Strong-Flower had warned Tuck about the danger of my getting chilled. In my weakened condition, he had said, a chest cold could easily develop into pneumonia and take my life.)

Tuck didn't know that the Lord was teaching me how to stand up against the enemy of sickness now, and I was learning fast. Jesus said He had come to give abundant life, and I was bound and determined to have it! Every day I was reading and memorizing the promises of healing and reminding myself, and Jesus, that He came to heal and to save me. I knew He would do what He promised, so I wasn't worried about getting pneumonia.

Before starting his fire, Tuck lit several candles and put them around the room in safe places. "Do you know who's bringing your dinner tonight?" He asked the question without looking toward me.

"Friend Joy," I answered. "She phoned to say she'd be here if she had to come in by dogsled."

That reminded me of the radio announcer's threat of "impassable roads"—and another nagging worry was added to my burden of negative thoughts. *Suppose I get really sick and Tuck can't take me to the doctor—what then*?

Now Tuck was busy arranging the logs on the brass andirons. When he struck a match to light the fire, I prayed it would burn well on the first try. It did. The wood caught rapidly, and the warm glow from the fireplace cheered my heart. The whole room began to take on a mellow warmth. I caught a faint scent of the eucalyptus young Friend June had put in an earthen jar near the hearth.

"Suppose we have a little prayer-and-praise time together," I suggested brightly. In my heart I really *was* grateful to God, but my timing was definitely off.

"Helen, can you please *wait*? At least until I take off my overcoat and wet shoes, before they freeze on me!"

The words stung, bringing tears to my eyes. Even if Tuck was looking (which he wasn't), he couldn't possibly see them in the darkened room. *Why don't you make him more sensitive to my needs*? I complained to the Lord. *He doesn't even care how sick I feel*. This time, I heard no reply. Glum-faced, I lay stiff and silent.

As the fire began to burn steadily, Tuck lit the old red hurricane lamp and placed it on a table. As its light flickered and danced about the room, he finally came over to me. *He'll apologize and kiss me,* I thought. *Then we'll be all right.* Again I was disappointed. My husband was still preoccupied.

"Where is a hat of some kind and a pair of gloves you can wear?" he asked.

"A *hat*?" I asked, astonished at his request. I hadn't worn a hat in years.

"Yes. If the power stays off, you'll need it to keep your head warm. You can sleep on the sofa in front of the fire tonight. *Maybe* we have enough wood to keep you warm the rest of the night, if I pile it on the hearth and get it dried out before we try to burn it. But you'll need some warm clothes, even under the blankets."

I scrambled around in my memory, trying to think where he might find a hat. "Look in the top drawer of my dresser. There's an old wool toboggan or something . . ." My voice trailed off into nothingness as Tuck turned and headed for the bedroom. Soon I could hear him rummaging around in the never-never land of my dresser drawers.

Tears filled my eyes, and shame filled my heart as I remembered what Jesus had told me in the hospital about Tuck's being covered with the vestments of God's love. *Lord, please don't let him see me crying,* I begged. My pity party over, I could again hear the Lord speaking to me tenderly: *He isn't insensitive to Me, daughter, nor to you. He's just doing his Father's will in taking care of his bride.*

I understood why Jesus had chosen the word *bride* in His description of Tuck's actions. It symbolized His own love for the Bride of Christ—His tenderness, grace, and mercy extended toward all believers. That love fills the pages of the New Testament.

I chose Tuck for you, He continued, *because I knew he would take good care of you all the rest of your lives. He's handpicked for your particular need—and you are chosen for his need.*

Now I was weeping tears of gratitude. How gracious of the Lord to make me feel wanted and needed, as well as immeasurably blessed! Throwing off the covers and struggling up from the couch, I went in search of my husband. I could hardly wait to put my arm around his neck and hug him—but when he saw me coming down the hall he admonished me for leaving the fire.

Making no protest, I obediently returned to the couch. Tuck came over to me, thrust the silly-looking toboggan squarely on my head, and handed me the brand-new, bright-green gardening gloves he had brought. Without a word, I pulled them on.

Next, Tuck helped me to my feet and wrapped his huge woolen bathrobe around me, tying the belt in a big knot. After I had sunk down onto the sofa, he covered me with so many blankets that I felt like a mummified papoose, wrapped and strapped into immobility.

"Now stay under those covers and don't get up again," he commanded. Childlike, I obeyed—thankful that only Tuck was there to see me in my ludicrous attire.

The huge knot of the bathrobe belt bit into my side, gradually numbing it, and the heat from the fireplace was fast becoming a major threat to my welfare. I felt weak and helpless. As soon as Tuck went outside to look for more firewood, I struggled to free myself from captivity. Deciding I would rather faint from effort than from heat stroke, I began peeling off blankets one by one, hoping Tuck wouldn't catch me at it. Survival was of first importance.

Tuck was still outside when Joy drove up—not in a dogsled but in a car equipped with tire chains. She came into the house stamping snow from her boots and laughing gleefully. After going to the kitchen to deposit the huge, steaming tray of food she was carrying, she came to speak to me before preparing our supper. Ignoring the hat, gloves, and oversized bathrobe, she spoke words of encouragement and love.

"Things are getting better all the time! I saw men working on the utility poles outside. Some of our friends telephoned the power company to report your special need for service, so they're hurrying to repair the lines leading to your house."

Again, tears flooded my eyes. I felt almost overwhelmed by the goodness of my heavenly Father and of the friends He had given me. As I watched Joy moving about in the kitchen, the tears of gratitude spilled over and ran down my cheeks. Until now, I hadn't fully understood the significance of the promise the Lord gave me at the very beginning of my hospital stay: "Before you call, I will answer"(see Isaiah 65:24).

I knew that the women in my Tuesday-morning prayer group had met together several times while I was in the hospital, in order to plan for my present and future needs to be met. Friend Vicky told me later that God had directed their planning, as they wrote down exactly what Tuck and I would need, then made out menus and schedules for meals, housework, and laundry. They assured Tuck that one of the women would bring lunch to me every day, and that a hot dinner would be provided for us both at night. As it turned out, so many friends and neighbors also brought food that Tuck was able to freeze enough for meals far into the future.

After arranging things so that Tuck could easily serve our supper when we were ready for it, Joy had a prayer with us before she left. "Helen is already a modern-day Job," she told the Lord. "Could you please do something special for her before the night is over?"

She had been gone less than an hour when the lights popped on in our house! Looking around the neighborhood from our side porch, Tuck could see only darkness in the other homes—but in our house the hum of the refrigerator was distinctly heard, and the furnace was sending heat into all the cold rooms. How we praised God! We didn't try to understand His mercy to us; we just thanked Him for it and asked Him to show the same mercy to our neighbors. Then Tuck extinguished the hurricane lamp and the candles.

When we had finished our good meal, and the flames had died out in the fireplace, Tuck helped me into bed in the guest room. Then he sat down in the rocking chair beside me and thrust a thermometer into my mouth, at the same time asking how I felt. He didn't wait until I could remove the thermometer to answer his question, but immediately got up and went to check and recheck things around the house. As I lay back in the guest-room four-poster, I felt the Holy Spirit prompting me to pray.

God, please bring me on through to a victorious Christian life, no matter how much testing it takes. Keep revealing the weak areas until You can make them strong.

And Lord, I ask your richest blessings upon my husband. Forgive me for not appreciating him just as he is. Forgive my ingratitude and my "murmuring." Help me to love him enough to give him what he needs: comfort, assurance, appreciation. Lord, I am sorry for my sins toward this head of our house that You have given me. Forgive me now and lift us up in our spirits, by Your precious Spirit. Amen.

Although I didn't hear a response from the Lord, I remembered with special gratitude the words from Romans 8:1: "There is therefore now no condemnation to them which are in Christ Jesus."

When Tuck returned to check my temperature, I confessed my sins of selfishness to him too and received his good-night kiss of forgiveness. That evening, we had passed through a crisis that had nothing to do with a snowstorm. Without realizing my increasing dependency, I had begun to expect too much from Tuck. It had taken another hard lesson to get me back into harmony with my husband and with the Lord. *Lord, must it always be this way? When will I ever learn—become mature, steadfast?*

As the door closed softly behind Tuck, I carefully eased my arm across the sheet in search of a comfortable position. Now I could let the tears flow freely. Into the darkness I whispered, "Lord, I can't, but You can—in me. What I lack, You in me will supply. I yield. Amen."

21

Doctors, Friends, and Strangers

The following Monday, I had an appointment with Dr. Strong-Flower. When Tuck told him about my being discharged from the hospital with a fever of 102, he expressed surprise and seemed concerned. After taking my temperature and examining me, he told Tuck to take me immediately to our family physician, and to let him (Dr. Strong-Flower) see me again the next morning. In my foolishness and because I felt so bad, I begged my husband not to take me to Faithful Family Physician's office. Against his better judgment, Tuck gave in to my argument that bed rest was the thing I needed most at that moment.

The next day I was much sicker. It was all I could do to dress, get into the car, and ride to Dr. Strong-Flower's office. With a serious expression and in uncharacteristic silence, he conducted a brief examination, then told me to come into his office after I was dressed. When I got there, I was surprised to find Tuck with him. Both men had grave faces.

Talking to my husband as though I weren't present, Dr. Strong-Flower said, "I don't think your wife is taking this thing seriously enough. She's had an extremely serious operation and is a long way from being recovered. She has very little resistance to infection, and if this respiratory infection progresses to pneumonia, it could be disastrous.'' Although his voice was serious, his tone was kind.

I sat there mute, feeling like an inanimate object being discussed. For a fleeting moment, fear gripped my heart. I knew God was in control, but I also knew I had been disobedient in not going to Family Physician yesterday. After sending up a quick prayer of confession—*Forgive me, Lord, and redeem*—I apologized to Dr. Strong-Flower for being uncooperative.

Then and there, Dr. Strong-Flower called our doctor and set up an appointment for me within the hour. There was some discussion as to whether I should be readmitted to the hospital; but Dr. Strong-Flower finally decided to allow me to go home on a trial basis.

Convinced by Dr. Strong-Flower's obvious concern and by my own physical condition, I was beginning to take the whole thing seriously. I felt so bad that I didn't see how I could possibly get back in the car, make a trip to the hospital laboratory to have blood drawn, then undress again in order to be examined by another doctor. *God, where will the strength come from*? Even as I asked the question, of course, I knew the answer.

Tears come easily these days, I thought, as my eyes filled and overflowed. Dr. Strong-Flower appeared not to notice, but his voice was kind as he instructed Nurse True-Calling to make an immediate appointment for me at the hospital laboratory.

Tuck helped me with my coat, holding the sleeves out wide so I could slip my arms halfway into them. Slowly we walked out to the parking lot. After opening the car door, my husband stood close while I eased myself inside. He was learning to avoid all unnecessary contact with my body.

As I laid my head back against the headrest, I called on Jesus for His supernatural strength, telling Him I was counting on Him to get me through all the morning's activities. I knew that was the only way I was going to make it. *Why, God,* why? *Haven't I had enough*? I closed my eyes and wept bitterly.

Even as the tears rolled down my cheeks, I realized anew that, no matter what the cost to me, I would still choose God's highest will for my life. My heart had long ago made that decision. The realization brought fresh comfort. Again I reminded myself, *I don't really have to understand any of this. Just trust Him.*

Suddenly I heard Him speak to my anguished heart: *Let the words of* My *mouth and the meditations of* your *heart be the same now, daughter. I will restore health unto thee, and I will heal thee of thy wounds.*

My heart almost burst with fresh joy. I knew then that I would be healed, just as I had read in Jeremiah 30:17: "For I will restore health unto thee, and I will heal thee of thy wounds, saith the Lord. . . ."

Hugging God's promise to myself, I survived the trips to the laboratory and to Faithful Family Physician's office. He checked me, gave Tuck prescriptions, and sent me home with orders for complete bed rest. That was like throwing Br'er Rabbit into the briar patch. I could hardly *wait* to get back under the covers! I would meditate on Jeremiah continually, but for now, just rest.

Back home at last, Tuck helped me undress and get into pajamas. I soon fell asleep, exhausted but full of joy. I now had God's promise of full restoration! Praise His wonderful name! *I can't wait to discuss it with Tuck when I get rested and can rejoice with him in it!*

It was late afternoon when the phone rang, waking me from my nap.

"Anybody home?" inquired a cheery voice. "We're on our way with your rations. Be there in half an hour." It was our friends, the Royals.

An hour later, the phone rang again. "We're lost," announced the same voice, now slightly less cheery. "Can't find your subdivision."

"Why don't I meet you at the intersection of Six Forks and Old Wake Forest Roads?" Tuck suggested. "I hate to think of you wandering around on these slick streets."

I hated to think of Tuck's starting out in the dark on the same slick streets, just to bring our dinner home; but he was gone before I could finish my protest.

As time dragged slowly by, I prayed fervently for Royal Couple and for my husband. Finally the flash of car lights in the carport announced that Tuck was safely home. I was surprised to hear his familiar chuckle as he opened the door; I had expected him to return wet, cold, and miserable. Instead, he came into the room grinning from ear to ear, a huge wicker basket slung over one arm and a large thermos bottle in the other hand.

"You'll never believe what the Royals went through to get this food to us," he said. After unloading his bounty in the kitchen and removing his overcoat and hat, he told me a most astounding story.

It seems that Royal Couple, on their way to meet Tuck, hit a patch of ice that caused their car to skid. After turning completely around, it spun back into place on the highway, in perfect formation with the flow of traffic.

When they reached the intersection where Tuck was waiting for them, the Royals were praising God for His protection and laughing heartily over the condition of our dinner. "Tuck," said Friend Royal, "if you all want this food, you're sure gonna have to help us scrape these English peas out of the Missus' boot tops and find Helen's fried chicken somewhere between the back seat and the floormat. When we hit that patch of ice, her dinner took off and we haven't seen it since."

Tuck climbed into their car, and the three of them scrabbled around collecting food from all its hiding places. Everything that looked edible they put back into the picnic basket.

Our dinner that night might not have been the most sanitary repast we ever enjoyed, but the seasonings of love and gratitude and good humor made it highly palatable. Those same seasonings, I'm sure, hastened my recovery from the virus that had complicated my convalescence and threatened my life.

After Tuck left for work the next morning, I took out my Bible and began to read the familiar words from Psalm 103, verses 1–3: "Bless the Lord, O my soul: and all that is within me, bless his holy name. . . . Forget not all his benefits: who forgiveth all thine iniquities, who healeth all thy diseases."

Right there, I stopped and personalized those life-giving words:

> Bless the Lord, O my lymph glands: and all that is within them, bless His holy name.
>
> Bless the Lord, O my bloodstream, and forget not all His benefits:
>
> Who forgiveth all thine iniquities, who healeth all thy cancer.

Thereafter, I sang those words aloud every day as I came before the Lord to praise and worship Him, and to let Him give me new truths from His Word.

One of the cornerstones of my faith is Romans 8:28: "And we know that all things work together for good to them that love God, to them who are the called according to his purpose." When I asked God to show me what good was being accomplished by my suffering, He drew my attention to the *following* verse: "For whom he did foreknow, he also did predestinate *to be conformed to the image of his Son . . .*" (italics added).

Obviously, no higher good can come to a follower of Christ than to be made like Him. But if this human clay is ever to bear even a remote resemblance to the Savior, the divine Sculptor will have to subject it to a lot of pressure and some sharp instruments—the scalpel, for example.

I accept that, Lord, and I trust You with my whole heart. I know that whatever comes into my life is part of Your plan for my highest good. Nothing can touch me except it first pass through Your hand. That knowledge keeps me safe and confident. Thank You for showing me why You don't always spare me suffering—and thank You too that You are always with me in *my suffering.*

One morning I put a question to the Lord: *As I convalesce, how can I spend my hours to please You?*

Softly, His words came to my waiting heart: *Return to that forgotten way of praying through the daily newspapers.* I knew just what He meant. Turning to the table at my elbow, I picked up our Raleigh morning paper and began. First, the world headlines: Israel and America—how they need prayer! Local news items, feature stories—they each tell about real people who have needs that should be lifted up to the Lord: brides and grooms beginning new homes, people dying, babies being born.

Lord, I'm sure going to be an extremely busy getting-well patient, I said to Him joyfully. *Hallelujah*!

Every morning and afternoon after that, when the newspapers were delivered, I spent part of my time praying through them, asking God's blessings for the people and situations I read about. One day I asked the Lord why I was spending so much time praying for strangers, and He told me it was because some of them didn't have anyone else to pray for them. Then He reminded me that He loves everyone and is not willing to give anyone up or see anyone perish (see 2 Peter 3:9). Tears came spontaneously when He whispered to my heart, *I've limited myself to the prayers of humanity, Helen. Pray for these people—strangers to you, but not to Me—so that I can act on their behalf.*

God created the whole world; yet He has need of praying Christians. What an amazing God!

He soon showed me something amazing about His *love*: The more

I let Him love strangers through me, the more love He gave me to share with my friends and family—especially with my husband.

As I continued to pray daily for my "newspaper people," I learned to pray more effectually for my loved ones. And I began to see things happen as a result of these more earnest prayers. Having always been a firm believer in talking things over with God, now I found my prayers taking on a deeper meaning.

Next, He began to teach me how to pray without ceasing. Sometimes I would be awakened during the night by the earnestness of my own praying in the Spirit. I became increasingly aware of the deep, hidden, inner needs of others, sometimes without a word being spoken by them. The Ephesians Scripture, "Praying always with all prayer and supplication in the Spirit, and watching thereunto with all perseverance and supplication for all saints" (6:18) soon held rich new meaning for me. I was learning to pray. *Really* pray.

As my interest in all this heightened, I began to study books on prayer: how to pray more effectively, how to seek God's will in prayer, how to persevere in prayer, how to pray and not to faint (quit). Life became brighter as I was lifted out of the world of self-involvement into the larger world of need around me. Our home became a worldwide arena instead of four walls built around *me*. The horizons lifted from "just us four, and no more," to encompass first my neighborhood, then my city and state, and finally the nations of the world. I found myself stretched out into realms of prayer that I had not known existed.

As I read the Bible aloud and meditated on the verses, the Lord encouraged me to be productive right where I was; in the very circumstances of sickness, weakness, and aloneness, to press on in prayer continually. *Forget yourself. Trust Me with you. Forget even the pain. Press on, daughter. Press on to Me*!

The daily seasons of prayer increased, bringing fresh courage, renewed hope in living. I did not realize it at the time, but all this praying for others was producing healing in my own body, soul, and spirit because the life of Christ was flowing through me and out into the world around, as I lay on the couch in the den day by day, talking out loud to God. I knew He was listening!

As the flow of His Spirit was bringing new life into me, building up my immunity system, and stimulating healing, gradually I noticed that I was beginning to feel better. One day as I read aloud the words from Isaiah 58:5–11, Jesus personalized them to the deepest part of my thirsty soul:

> Is it not to deal thy bread to the hungry, and that thou bring the poor that are cast out to thy house? when thou seest the naked, that thou cover him, and that thou hide not thyself from thine own flesh? (v.7)

I meditated intently on the words. "What do You mean, Lord? How can I deal bread to the hungry now? I can't even cook for Tuck and me."

As I waited before Him, the meaning was made very clear to my hungry heart: In dealing out the bread of prayer to the people written about in the newspapers, I was providing an avenue for God to bless the hungry in spirit; in praying for the poor, I was bringing their needs into my home; prayer was clothing the street people who were so often on my mind.

One day He reminded me that, because of my illness, I had neglected to send some of our warm, woolen coats, sweaters, and blankets to the poor, so Tuck gathered them up and took them to the Rescue House. I then began to write short notes to long-forgotten relatives. Some of them needed encouragement, and others had never met Jesus, so I introduced them by mail. Gathering Christmas pamphlets and tracts, we stuffed envelopes, as my strength permitted, and Tuck mailed them out to whoever came to mind. I took the telephone book and prayed through it for names to which to send the literature. It seemed a hopeless task, but we finally got everything mailed out.

The moments of boredom and deadly self-evaluation soon vanished. I don't remember when they went; I was too busy about my Father's business to notice.

One day, in a renewed act of self-surrender, I raised my hands to the Lord as I lay on the sofa in the family room, and wave upon wave of His Glory swept over my soul. I was impressed that there is no possible way to outgive this marvelous God of ours. If we try to bless others, He multiplies the blessing back to us many times over.

As I continued reading in Isaiah 58, the words of verse 8 seemed to leap off the page right into my heart:

> Then shall thy light break forth as the morning, *and thine health shall spring forth speedily:* and thy righteousness shall go before thee; the glory of the Lord shall be thy rereward. (italics added)

I was being healed! Again the waves of His glory flooded my being. Right then and there I got so happy, I could hardly contain myself. Because I hadn't shouted since I was Head Cheerleader in high school, I had forgotten how, but I was so full of joy that I almost exploded. What had begun as a simple act of obedience was unfolding a whole new world of blessing for me. What a God!

I read the promises of God over and over again into the vacant room:

> And if thou draw out thy soul to the hungry, and satisfy the afflicted soul, then shall thy light rise in obscurity, and thy darkness be as the noon day. (v.10)

The sun was coming up in my life once again, and nothing could prevent His light. *I was being healed.* Just as He had promised me on New Year's Day at Virginia Beach! Lying on the sofa, unable to rise without strain and pain, I didn't appear to be well, but my spirit man knew that the Lord Jesus had completed the job and that I was to walk it out with confidence. It wasn't by works of my righteousness that I merited His favor, but by His mercy and grace.

Scripture praises flowed from the Spirit of God through my lips and back to Him. The healing process in my body had quickened. What a plan! The tap of His healing mercies had been turned by His hand as I had been praying for others. I remembered reading in the Book of Job about the same thing: "And the Lord turned the captivity of Job, when he prayed for his friends" (42:10).

I raised my voice in singing and praise, worshiping Him. I sang from the Psalms, remembering the words from learning them in grammar school. How I had hated to memorize! But how wonderful that I had been forced to learn God's Word! The floodtide of worship and praise reached new heights, flowing and ebbing at His will.

How long I lay praising Him I do not know, but when it was over, I knew that a stream of healing virtue had filled my being. Finally, I lay back on the pillows exhausted, but filled with the awareness of His presence with me. I would be made whole. Maybe not today. Perhaps not even tomorrow. But I had His Word that healing would come. It was already on its way.

22

A Love Story

It was wonderful being back home together, Tuck and I, and I prayed we would never again be separated. Being together made us content, even happy. The recurrent theme of our prayers was gratitude for the Lord's blessings—especially, at this time, the friends who provided so bountifully for our material and emotional needs.

The hardest thing we had to deal with now was the every-other-day routine of going to Dr. Strong-Flower's office to have my incisions drained and my wounds bandaged. Jesus had told me in the hospital not to anticipate anything—not even for half an hour. This word of wisdom, together with His promise to answer even before I called, helped me get through this trying period. I learned to trust Him for the moment, without looking ahead—and He never once failed me. I was always ready, *by faith,* for whatever came. When fear or panic or pain threatened to overwhelm me, I knew victory would be right on the heels of each trial of faith. God always keeps His word.

My appointments were usually around 2:30 in the afternoon. On those days, Tuck worked through his lunch hour so that he could take me to the doctor. The procedure was painful, and it was comforting to know that Tuck was out in the waiting room praying for me.

On each visit, long needles were jabbed deep into my side to drain my wounds, and I could hear the blood as it spurted from the syringe, hitting the enameled pan. *Lord,* I prayed, *this is nothing to the pain You felt when the soldier pierced Your side on the cross. This is to prolong life, but the spear was thrust into Your side to hasten death.*

From the beginning, I formed the habit of drawing on my memory bank of Bible promises while I lay on the examining table and the doctor and nurse worked on me. I usually repeated the verses in my mind, but when the pain seemed unbearable I sometimes got a bit audible. Hearing His Word and promises spoken aloud helped me bear the ordeals. So did talking to Jesus about it—praising Him and sometimes singing softly to Him. On my first few visits, Dr. Strong-Flower would occasionally pause to ask me what I had said or the nurse would ask if I needed something. After a while, they became accustomed to my way of dealing with the pain, and nobody seemed to mind.

God had surely chosen my helpers well. They were understanding, patient, and kind, and I loved them both so much that they were bound to feel it. Often we talked freely about the Lord. Dr. Strong-Flower told me that he *treated* patients, but it was God who healed them. Before I finished my series of postoperative visits, I brought him a modern translation of the Bible and Nurse True-Calling a good devotional book.

One frosty day, when the temperature had reached a new low, we were driving toward the office for my appointment. Ill with another throat infection, I sat hunched over in the front seat, my eyes closed. I was trying hard not to cry. Apparently sensing my discomfort, Tuck reached across the car to pat my hand.

As we waited at an intersection for the traffic signal to change, I heard the Lord speak softly, *Open your eyes.*

I didn't obey. *The effort is too great,* I thought.

Open your eyes. I want you to see her.

Curious now, I opened my eyes and looked out the window on my side of the car. On a bench at the bus stop, a young girl was sitting alone. She looked almost frozen, but I could tell she was praying for me. The glory of the Lord surrounded her sweet young face, and when my eyes fleetingly met hers through the car window, we both smiled. Immediately the light changed and Tuck drove on, but the blessing I received from that young woman lingered throughout my office visit.

For weeks, I had dreaded seeing what I looked like underneath the bandages. I knew the sight would not be pretty, and I was afraid I might not be able to face it triumphantly. One day, Dr. Strong-Flower must have read my thoughts, for he said softly, "Take your time; we won't force . . ."

Reaching over, I patted his hand. "Haven't you got some pictures in one of your books to show me how I'll look?"

"Those pictures look worse than the actuality," Nurse True-Calling said, thus bringing the conversation to an end.

I realized that eventually I would have to face the reality hidden beneath those clean white bandages, but I was thankful it wouldn't be today. I wished it had all disappeared, so the ugly part would have escaped my inspection. I knew that someday it would be healed completely, but for now I must bear up under the suspense.

As my visits to Dr. Strong-Flower were stretched further and further apart, I knew the day would soon come when he would make the dreaded announcement. Sure enough, as I lay on the examining table one February afternoon, he said to me, "Mrs. Tucker, I think it is time for me to teach you to dress your wounds yourself. Then you won't have to continue these visits any longer."

Terror hit my heart. *Out, Satan, in the name of Jesus Christ. I resist the spirit of fear. I'm a child of God, and you have no place in me.* The fear left me immediately, but still I made the cowardly suggestion that he teach my husband instead.

"Let's not ask him to do that. You can do this for yourself now."

How could I? I thought. I hated the sight of wounds and hurt places. Even when my little sons cut their fingers, I usually fainted before I got the Band-Aids and Mercurochrome ready.

Zero hour, I thought.

Suddenly, without warning, a dam broke somewhere within my heart, allowing the tears that had been forcibly held back before Doctor and Nurse to flow freely. I was no longer trying to be brave or to give a good "Christian witness." I just bawled and didn't care who saw me. I know the Lord must have been glad for me to be rid of my self-effort to appear noble and righteous. *Lord, let them all see me cry!*

"This is an emotional event; let it all come out." Dr. Strong-Flower's voice was gentle. "We'll wait until your next visit to show you how to change your bandages."

Once the flow of tears had started, there seemed to be no stopping them. I was still crying when Tuck and I reached home. He had not seen me cry uncontrollably like this over my illness—not even at the first discovery of the lump—and it disturbed him greatly. Coming around to my side of the car, he carefully guided me into the house.

"What do I care if I'm a coward?" I sobbed. "You might as well see me cry too. It's bad enough to be the patient, but now I've got to be my own doctor, too, and dress 'dem wounds.' "

When I said that, I glanced up at Tuck and we both burst out laughing, even though the tears were still running down my cheeks. Because we couldn't embrace, we just stood inside the door and grinned at each other.

"Scars fade away," Tuck said finally, "and Dr. Strong-Flower says reconstructive surgery is possible. Besides, you have a beautiful face." With that, he leaned over to kiss my cheek. It didn't matter if his love was blind; for the moment, it helped me and gave me courage to come to a private decision: I would face the bandages and accept however I looked. Vaguely, I wondered if Tuck could accept me too. Then I remembered the Scripture verse that says, "Love never fails" (1 Corinthians 13:8 NKJV)—and I knew that the love God had put between us was strong enough to pass that test.

For both Tuck and me, one of the most trying aspects of the convalescent period was having to sleep in separate rooms. It was hard to be deprived of that physical closeness, the intimacy of impromptu bedtime chitchat. As my strength gradually returned, I felt a growing desire to put my arms around Tuck and just hold him close. I knew he felt the same way, but we had to be careful because of my wounded body.

One afternoon when I came out of the guest room, he was walking down the hall just in front of me. The back of his head has always been especially precious to me; I think it is shaped beautifully. The blue sweater he was wearing—the one with his initials on it that I had given him for Christmas—accentuated the silvery sheen of his hair. My heart just turned over with love for him, and I asked him to wait. Stopping, he turned around and looked at me with love in his eyes.

"I have such a desire just to touch you," I said. "If you'll stand still, I believe we can work it out. . . . Don't try to face me. You might forget and put your arm around me. Let me just love you my way."

Obediently he stood still, his arms straight down at his sides like a toy soldier. I reached one arm around his waist—very gently, very carefully—and gave him a big bear hug. Oh, it was the most precious of love gestures! Putting my cheek on his shoulder, I nestled against him, content just to be close to him. Tears came down my cheeks and sank into his heather blue sweater, but he didn't move. We stood there silently as long as I had the strength to stand; then Tuck helped me back into bed. As he turned to pull the sheets up to my chin, I saw that *his* face too was moist. During all this time, not one word had been spoken. Words weren't necessary.

Lying there in the guest-room bed, I looked back over the years of our marriage and saw a marvelous love story: the love of God molding two people together through the ups and downs, mountain peaks and valleys of their shared experience. We hadn't always understood His dealings with us—but we knew we could count on His love for us and on the love He had given us for each other.

Even as I wondered what the next few years would bring, I knew He would continue to lead us and mold us in the future as He had in the past.

23

A Winter Weekend at the Beach

"Dr. Strong-Flower, I've just got to ask you something." For once, I made no attempt at levity. Usually, I forced myself to have some light conversation with Dr. Strong-Flower and Nurse True-Calling on each visit; but today I was serious as I lay on the hard leather examining table.

"What's that, young lady?"

There's nothing like being called "young" to build up the confidence of any aging female—so I continued boldly. "What effect will my unhealed scars have on my husband, do you suppose?"

Being a very tactful man, my doctor was looking up at the ceiling as though it required his undivided attention at that moment. Gratefully, I closed my eyes and waited.

"Mrs. Tucker, from what I've observed of your husband, you don't have a thing to worry about. The way he's hung around this office should be enough to put all your worries to rest."

That brought a smile from Nurse True-Calling and me. Tuck had continued to take me to the doctor's office long after I needed him to do so. Friends had offered to drive me, but Tuck had been reluctant to relinquish the responsibility—until Dr. Strong-Flower eventually assured him I would be fine without his bird-dog attention.

Since I had given him the opening, Dr. Strong-Flower suggested that I now take a look under my bandages. I sensed that he had been building up to this moment for some time. He wanted me to face the inevitable, conquer any fear, and learn to take care of my wounds. I had repeatedly delayed this hour—but now I could postpone it no longer. Summoning all my courage, I lifted my head from the pillow and took a quick peek.

Lord! My whole side seemed to be missing. I sank back down on the examining table and said aloud, "My God! My God!"

For a while there was silence in the room, as Dr. Strong-Flower began replacing the bandages. During that interval fear struck like a tornado. I began to tremble. *God, help me! I can't stand it! I'm so scared—so cold.*

"Get her a blanket." Dr. Strong-Flower's voice was calm, soft. I felt the cover fall gently across my legs. The trembling increased until my whole body was shaking. Nurse True-Calling held my hand while Dr. Strong-Flower continued to bandage the wounds. He kept talking, trying to reassure me, but I couldn't hear his words.

God, I pleaded silently. *God, God*! I knew my only help lay in Him. *Without You, I can't stand it. You'll have to take care of me. Please don't let me be so afraid. I'm so afraid*!

Immediately, help came from heaven in an unexpected way. The words of a song I had heard long ago dropped into my mind: "Stay laid back in His arms." I repeated the words over and over to myself. Gradually, peace came and the trembling stopped. The crisis was past.

Stay laid back in His arms. Like a refrain, the words kept running through my mind as Nurse True-Calling helped me get dressed. Gently, the assurance came to me that everything would be all right. I was no longer afraid.

When I returned home from the doctor's office, I discovered that my bandages were smaller. Cautiously, I peeked at the underside of my arm. The scars were worse than I had imagined!

"*Surely goodness and mercy shall follow me all the days of my life*" [Psalm 23:6]—*and that means while I'm looking in the mirror too. But Lord, whatever happens, please don't let Tuck feel sorry for me. I don't believe I can stand that kind of emotion.*

Although it was still very painful to move my arm, I faithfully continued my exercises—at the same time making longer inspections in front of my mirror each day. When it had become bearable for me to look at myself, I went into the family room one night and, without warning, showed my arm to Tuck. It wasn't the thing to do. He winced noticeably, then tried to hide it. His pain was very apparent. We didn't talk, and I quickly left the room.

Back in our bedroom, I held tightly to the edge of the dressing table with one trembling hand and fumbled for the chair with the other. I sank down heavily and put my head on the table. *Lord,* I thought, *I've had so many operations, so much anguish. What will I do? How will I make it through life? God!* Tears, torrents of tears, came.

I heard Tuck's footsteps coming down the hall. *Lord! Lord!* He came over to the dressing table and knelt down on the floor beside me. Wrapping his arms tightly around my legs and the chair, he wept silently. I leaned my head on top of his. We were facing another crisis together.

In the days that followed, Tuck continued to have difficulty looking at my arm—so I tried to keep it covered for a while. The next week, Dr. Strong-Flower removed the heavy bandages from my chest and replaced them with a smaller one. The extent of the surgery was now plainly visible. No more hiding. Determined to put an end to my own misery and to help Tuck bear the signs of my suffering, I decided on a bold plan.

As I prepared for bed that night, I rolled up the kimono sleeve of my robe, and holding my arm up in the air as high as possible, I walked into the family room—again without any warning. Silently, I stood before Tuck. When he looked up from his newspaper, his face momentarily registered unmistakable shock. Then he leaped from his chair, lifted my face in both his hands and said, "Praise You, Jesus! You gave me back her life." With that, he kissed me. The dreaded moment was past for a lifetime. Jesus had given us another victory.

When Tuck came home from work the following Thursday, I could sense that he was elated over something. He carefully hung his hat and coat in the closet, then came and sat beside me.

"How would you like to drive to Atlantic Beach and spend the weekend?" he asked, trying to suppress the excitement in his voice. "Charlie and Bernard have offered us their condominium at Coral Bay for a few days." Tuck's eyes were alight, his face glowing with pleasure.

Like my husband, I was delighted over the prospect of a change of scenery. The long ride to the beach seemed a bit ambitious for my strength; but if Tuck thought I could do it, I was willing to try. We planned the trip for the following weekend. I could hardly wait!

"I've never seen the ocean with snow on the beach," he said eagerly. "We'll take a pillow and blankets, so you can rest in the back seat."

We drove to the shore on a cold day bright with sunshine. I lay on the back seat of the automobile, looking out the windows at the few fleecy clouds in my line of vision. I was so glad to be alive, so grateful to God for my improving health! The intense blue of the sky thrilled my soul, making me feel that I was seeing the outskirts of heaven. I could sense God's presence everywhere around us. It was a glorious trip!

When we reached the condominium, Tuck escorted me along the weathered cedar walk leading into the corner building. After unlocking the azure-blue front door, he opened it wide and let me precede him up the short flight of steps leading to the second-floor living room. There we were greeted with a sparkling panorama of brilliant colors. Life surrounded us: glossy, bright-green plants grew from floor to ceiling; tropical fish—golden, pink, purple-tinted—darted freely about in crystal aquariums lined along the bookshelves. Rattan furniture was upholstered in brilliant shades of yellow and green, with an occasional burst of vibrant blue. Everything was beautiful! Sunlight patterns, reflecting the tossing blue waters of the Atlantic, played hide-and-seek on the walls of glass.

I was thrilled to feel alive again. Fascinated with the sea-life mobiles hanging from the cathedral ceiling, I walked around looking upward until Tuck called for me to come outside.

He opened the sliding glass doors, and we walked together onto the balcony that jutted out toward the ocean. From there we could hear the mighty roar of the waves as they crashed endlessly on the sandy shore. *What a beautiful place for You to bring us, Lord, as a gift of Your love, channeled through generous friends!* We were like small children joyous at play.

Although Nature's panorama seemed to be inviting us to "come out and see," a few minutes in the February wind made us glad to return to the warmth of the living room. While Tuck brought our suitcases inside, I made some hot chocolate to go with the chicken sandwiches we had brought along for our lunch. The aroma of chocolate filled the small kitchen and filtered into the living room, dispersing any feeling of strangeness. In almost no time, we were completely at home in our surroundings.

After eating our sandwiches and taking short naps, we sat together in the huge rattan lounging chairs, watching the ocean waves sparkle in the bright sunshine as they chased little grey sandpipers in and out of their swirling foam. We were content just to sit there holding hands. There was no need for conversation. I sensed that Tuck was experiencing the same deep gratitude I felt. We had been through some rough waters since our last weekend at the beach.

Could today be only February 23? It seemed as though years had passed since New Year's Eve. With a sigh, I vaguely wondered if I would ever adjust to my altered physical condition. All my waking hours were a constant fight against gravity. Without the help of someone's arm or a sturdy handrail, I felt as though my unbalanced body would catapult into space, spinning like a top. My chest seemed immobile, and my side was still numb and unfeeling.

"Do you suppose it will ever be sensitive again?" Almost without realizing it, I spoke the question aloud.

"*What* be sensitive, Helen?"

Momentarily, I had forgotten that my husband was not constantly aware of my thoughts.

"My side is so numb. If it got hurt, I wonder if I could even feel the pain. This truly concerns me at times."

Instead of answering, Tuck gave my hand a gentle squeeze. We had not spent much time discussing my operation and its aftermath. Years before, we had determined that our time could be used for better purposes than to hash and rehash details of illnesses.

Why do I allow such negative thoughts to intrude on our precious moments of happiness? I asked myself. *I must choose to be happy, regardless of my feelings. It's up to me—not God, not Tuck.*

I thought of something the Lord had told me years before, during another difficult period in my life: *Unless you are willing to come to the floor of the valley, experiencing all that I have for you there, you won't be fit to climb the mountain to Me.*

I had *been* to the floor of the valley, and I was on my way up the mountain—but I longed for the day when I would be free from sickness. How much longer would I have to pamper my body, to let physical limitations govern my activities and relationships?

"Lord," I prayed aloud, "Your Word says that You 'healed all that were sick' and that You 'took our infirmities, and bare our sicknesses' [see Matthew 8:16,17]. Right now, I claim healing as my divine right as Your child, and I trust You to manifest it in my body, in Your way and in Your time. But Lord, most important of all, help me always to keep YOU preeminent in my life. Thank You. Amen."

Tuck joined in with me: "Lord, I agree with my partner for us and our whole house. Praise You that You allowed Yourself to be wounded for our transgressions and bruised for our iniquities, and that with Your stripes we are healed!" (See Isaiah 53:5 and 1 Peter 2:24.)

"AMEN!" we declared in unison—so loudly that we both laughed.

"Come on, let's ride down the beach. You feel strong," Tuck affirmed. And so I did.

After a beautiful afternoon together, we returned to the condominium uplifted, our spirits refreshed. The wind blew the ocean spray toward our walls of glass, and we could sense the strength of the waves as they tossed about below us. In the warm and pleasant living room, we felt relaxed and happy. The view through the glass wall was a magnificent picture-postcard scene, the dunes below making picturesque white mountains against the backdrop of deep-blue seawater.

Taking out his copy of *The Living Bible,* Tuck read aloud from Psalm 93: "The mighty oceans thunder your praise. You are mightier than all the breakers pounding on the seashores of the world!"

We remained silent for a long time, filled with gratitude and content just to be with each other. It was a precious, divinely ordered moment.

Exhausted from the day's activities, I decided to turn in soon after supper. We planned to rise early and take a short automobile tour around Fort Macon, a Civil War fort near by. "We'll just take our time, go at your pace, and return when you get tired," Tuck had said. How good life felt to me!

After I was settled in bed, Tuck came over in his maroon corduroy robe and knelt beside me. Bowing his head, he began to pray aloud. The fervor of his prayer surprised me, for Tuck is usually calm and unemotional. *Tonight he is different,* I thought. *Perhaps it's because we haven't been so close together physically in a long time.*

I listened to the words my husband was saying to the Lord: thanking Him for sparing my life, healing me, guarding and taking care of me, being with me always. On and on he went, never once mentioning himself, but just praying for me. It was as though a dam had broken somewhere inside his heart, and its contents were spilling out before God. My tears fell down on his silver hair as he continued pouring his heart out to God.

Carefully, I lifted his head, cradling it with my good arm. He cautiously wrapped his arms around me, avoiding my bandaged side. Then he just held onto me. For hours, it seemed, he continued to hold me gently—almost reverently—in his arms while he continued to talk to God about me. My body began to ache and I longed to change position, but I dared not move. This love Tuck was demonstrating for me seemed so different—almost sacred.

Lord, what is this all about?

Softly, I heard Jesus speak to me: *This is a demonstration of My own love for My bride.*

I remembered that the Lord had touched on this subject the day I got home from the hospital. It must be very important for me to receive *this moment* the truth He wanted to reveal to me. *Explain it to me, Lord.*

He is loving you as I love the Church. He is giving himself up for you. He doesn't realize the importance of what he is doing, but he is sanctifying and cleansing you through the Word.

I knew He was referring to Ephesians 5:22-33, and a memory came vividly to mind. I had once put my hand on that very passage of Scripture, praying that my husband would some day love me with that Christ-like love. Now it was coming to pass. *Praise God from whom all blessings flow*!

On and on Tuck prayed. Sometimes he spoke clearly, every word distinct; sometimes his voice was barely audible—but I was sure Jesus was hearing him, even when I couldn't. My heart trembled at the fervor of his prayer.

"Lord, You died on Calvary to save her, to keep her, to mold her, to make her like Yourself. I pray, God, that with such love as this for her You will constantly bless Helen and keep her always close to Your heart. Never let her be afraid. Don't let any harm come to her, Jesus. I pray You, keep her always covered by Your precious blood. Lord, I claim this blood for her covering night and day, forever. Please don't let anything come nigh her to cause her hurt. Don't let her ever be far from You. Lord Jesus, Your Word says

You will never leave or forsake her. I count on You to do this for my wife. . . ."

Tuck's words continued to ebb and flow, sometimes melting into silent tears. Occasionally he brushed the sleeve of his robe across his face, without interrupting his prayer. At times his voice would break, tremble, or pause—but then the words continued with strength. Tuck seldom weeps; I was shaken by the depth of his emotion. I knew his unselfish prayers were reaching heaven.

Tuck stayed on his knees until I could no longer concentrate to follow his words. The aura of the Holy Spirit filled the whole bedroom. We were in the presence of the living Lord.

Finally Tuck was finished. He lifted his head and rose stiffly from his knees. Kissing me gently on the top of the head, he climbed into his bed without another word. I knew he was at peace.

Long after he had turned out the light, I lay listening to the distant sound of the surf and thanking God for His answer to my long-ago prayer for a husband who would love me as Christ loves the church. Deep within me, the assurance came that something fruitful for the Kingdom of God was being born from our suffering.

24
A Night on the Town

Our beach weekend marked the beginning of my return to normal living. The very next week, Friend Catherine was taking me to the doctor's office for a checkup, and she had invited me to go to lunch afterward. To my surprise and delight, I found it easy to get into her elegant new automobile unaided.

"This is one luxury I would truly like to have," I told her, glancing a bit disdainfully at my matronly-looking, navy-blue, seven-year-old sedan parked in the carport. I ran my hand over the soft, smooth leather of the seat and remembered that, before I went to the hospital, my skin had felt soft too. Now it felt like an old cattle hide that had baked too long in the Texas sun. *But it will heal,* I assured myself, settling down comfortably in Catherine's luxurious automobile.

We chatted happily as she drove me to Dr. Strong-Flower's office. He and Nurse True-Calling were pleased to see me looking so well, and his examination showed that I was progressing normally. "You can begin to take tub baths now," he told me. "Just be sure to keep the bandage dry."

I was smiling as I rejoined Catherine in the waiting room, after making an appointment for a return visit the next week. We told

Nurse True-Calling good-bye, then walked out to the parking lot and climbed into the car.

Watching Catherine as she turned the ignition key, I thought wistfully, *She's so lovely*. I stole a quick glance in the mirror on the back of the sun visor, wondering if I would ever be attractive again.

Catherine's voice broke into my thoughts. "Let's have lunch at Tea Gardens," she suggested. "It's my treat."

"Great!" was my enthusiastic reply. It felt *good* to be outside the house, enjoying a luncheon date with a friend.

At the oriental restaurant, we were shown to a small round table near the center of the room. Over a delicious lunch of egg roll and sweet-and-sour pork, with steaming pots of aromatic tea, we chatted and shared experiences, memories, and ideas for almost an hour. It seemed as though we picked up our conversation where we had left off the last time we had lunch together—several weeks before my surgery. It's always like this with true friends.

"Tell me all about the girls," I urged as we topped off our meal with slices of walnut cake. "The girls" were members of our Tuesday-Morning Prayer Group, who had been together for many years. Tuck and I were confident that their faithfulness was one of the main reasons I was making such a rapid recovery. God's love, continually flowing through their prayers and demonstrated in their acts of kindness, was bringing healing and restoration to my whole being.

After Catherine had brought me up to date on the friends I hadn't talked to recently, I whispered a spontaneous prayer of thanksgiving for them right there at the table. "Lord Jesus, how I praise You for faithful Christians! They are truly the cement that keeps this old world together." In chorus, we whispered "Amen!" grinning like two schoolgirls sharing a choice secret.

As Catherine drove me home after lunch, I told her about my exciting plans for the evening. "I have a heavy date with Tuck," I confided. "Our first real night out together since . . . you know—"

"I'm so glad, Helen! You're really making good progress."

After Catherine had let me out in my carport and her bright baby-blue automobile had slid down the street, I went into the house to get my beauty sleep and prepare for a very important evening. Tuck had made dinner reservations at the Carolina Country Inn for our first night out together. The thought of it made my heart sing. *Thirty-seven years married to this man, and still in love*! I smiled happily as I slipped on my robe and lay down for a brief nap to recharge my supply of energy before getting ready for my dinner date.

Awaking with an upsurge of joy in my spirit, I decided on a bold course of action: I was going to take a bath—a real *tub* bath! The mere thought of such a luxury thrilled me. No more "birdbaths" for me. I had Dr. Strong-Flower's permission to returned to civilized bathing.

I turned on the stereo, filling the house with relaxing music. It brought back instant memories. *I've been missing so many good things,* I thought. Sprinkling a generous quantity of bath-oil beads into the tub, I turned the tap and stood watching the soft swirls of warm water melt them, releasing their fragrance into the room. I couldn't wait to feel the warm water and let the bath oil soak into my parched skin. *So what if I'm still bandaged? I'll be OK if I just keep it dry; Dr. Strong-Flower said so.* Praising and thanking God, I danced a few wobbly, unsure steps in time to the music.

As I stepped into the tub, gratitude welled up within me for the Lord's goodness and mercy. *Lord, Your sweet, simple pleasures were all waiting for me—plus all the other treasures You've given us during my illness.* My mind went back to the wonderful friends who had continually, unselfishly showered their love on Tuck and me. The thought of their love warmed my heart.

While I was soaking, my mind turned to the question of what I should wear. My first night out on the town with Tuck was special—so important that I *had* to have everything just right. Somehow I must find an attractive dress that would hide my unusual front. What could I do to fill in the gap and disguise the bulky bandage?

Please help me, Jesus. Make me a wife Tuck can be proud of. I want him to be aware of me as he was when we were engaged. Besides that, I just plain, flat-out don't want to be ugly! I just can't wait for reconstructive surgery so I will be whole and sound again. Just like everybody else!

Well, back to what shall I wear *now*?

I knew I was asking a lot; but I also knew that the Lord cares about such seemingly small things. My personal happiness is important to the Father, though He will not let it interfere with His highest will for my life. I could expect Him to choose the best for His daughter (me) in everything. Since "everything" includes the mystery of suffering, it surely includes the proper attire for an important date with my husband.

I had luxuriated in the bathwater long enough! Time to start searching my closet for a soft, loose-fitting, *becoming* dress.

Finally, I chose a blue wool jumper, worn with a soft silken blouse. But what could possibly suffice underneath? Dr. Strong-Flower had briefly introduced the subject of breast forms and fittings, but said it was still too soon for me to try them.

Perhaps I could use one of Tuck's undershirts to fill in the front of my dress. Rummaging around in his bureau, I selected an old ragged one, softened by many washings. *That will be easy to fold,* I thought. Folding the undershirt flat, I placed it gently against my bandages before putting on my bra and blouse. It looked awful! My whole front was misshapen. One side of the blouse was filled out naturally; the other hung limp, looking as if someone had ironed me out with a flatiron.

Lord! What to do? I *refused* to feel sorry for myself. Snatching out the undershirt, I crumpled it into a smooth, round ball; then, closing my eyes tight, I thrust it into my bra cup over the bandage. The blouse fitted beautifully!

I just had time to finish dressing and applying my makeup before Tuck got home. Stealing a glance in the hall mirror as I went to meet him, I was surprised to see what a good job the Lord had done with me. Tuck told me I looked "beautiful" and "vibrant." I didn't believe a word of it but loved hearing him say it.

The long drive to the inn was relaxing. Tuck and I were silent for the most part, content to be together, sensing that this was a new beginning for us. Surely we could never be quite the same as before, but the Lord could make life even richer now that we had come victoriously through our trial by cancer.

The lovely old inn with its authentic antique furnishings seemed to be especially elegant that night. With surprising sureness, I walked up the winding mahogany staircase and entered the dining room beside my husband. As the waiter was seating us, I commented to Tuck that the silver reflected the candlelight with a special brilliance—just for us tonight. He smiled at my flight of fancy, but agreed with my sentiments.

After he had ordered our meal, a string quintet strolled by our table and stopped to play "Intermezzo," a song we had chosen for our wedding. I smiled to think that Tuck had requested it on this particular occasion.

Laughter came easily as we ate our melon cup. *How smoothly we can make the transition from grief to joy,* I thought happily. The pheasant under glass with Queen Anne sauce was delicious. We ate leisurely, savoring every mouthful and every minute of this special evening. I felt relaxed, happy, comfortable.

Not until we were well into the entree did I become aware that some kind of problem was beginning to develop in my chest area. Soon I knew that something was definitely amiss. Glancing down, I discovered to my dismay that my makeshift bosom had shifted. The borrowed undershirt had escaped from its moorings and was now resting gently against my neck, producing an unmistakable bulge under the high collar of my blouse.

Unbelievable! For a moment, I was shaken. Panic thoughts bombarded my mind: *What if someone notices? What shall I do—sit still or make a hasty exit to the ladies' room? Can I fix it, once I get in there alone?*

After a few miserable minutes, my sense of humor came to the rescue. The audacity of that T-shirt, to produce such an unsightly, misplaced bulge among all these elegant surroundings! Gradually, panic receded. Snickering, I alerted Tuck, showing him with my eyes where he was to look. His glance traveled appreciatively downward until he beheld the phenomenon. Then his face registered unbelief, followed by shock. *Sotto voce,* I explained to him my creative solution to the problem of my lopsided appearance—and when he saw I wasn't upset, we had a good laugh together.

I glanced around the room to see if others were watching, but no one else seemed aware of my dilemma. Since we certainly didn't want to attract attention, we soft-pedaled our mirth. It wasn't easy.

Still quietly savoring our joke, we finished our flame bananas and caramel sauce while Tuck's undershirt nestled confidingly against my neck. When the delicious meal was over and the waiter brought our check on its little silver tray, I glanced up at him and smiled. It really didn't matter if he noticed the odd bulge under my collar.

When we rose to go, I held my head high and walked out of the inn just as confidently as if my anatomy were properly distributed. A bulgy undershirt seemed a small matter in comparison to the largeness of God's blessings. Tonight I had learned for sure that romance wasn't dead; it had just been waiting in the wings.

We emerged from the inn to find a full moon shining brightly on the Carolina countryside, sending little shafts of light shimmering across the curving driveway. As Tuck and I drove along the highway leading home, my heart sang with happiness. I sensed that my husband too was filled with joy and fresh hope. He held my hand loosely all the way home, not letting go until he had to make the sharp turn into the driveway. Our first evening "on the town" had been an unqualified success.

That night, our quiet time with the Lord before we went to bed was especially sweet. We knew in our hearts that one more period of testing was past and a wonderful new beginning had been granted us. His Bible open to 1 John 4:4, Tuck read the words aloud: "Greater is he that is in you, than he that is in the world."

Triumphantly, I added, "CANCER, YOU BEHOLD JESUS!"

25

Coronation

When the weather moderated, Dr. Strong-Flower told me to take daily outdoor walks and to push against my physical weakness. With every effort, my body grew stronger.

I learned that it helped to praise God while I was doing my arm exercises. I pictured myself as being one of the priests who went into the sanctuary and lifted up holy hands to bless the Lord (see Psalm 134:2). Although the exercise was painful, it helped me to regain full use of my arm. At the same time, the praises I sent up to God helped me to regain "the joy of the Lord"—and that strengthened my spirit as well as my body (see Nehemiah 8:10).

By summertime, I was making rapid progress toward full recovery—and with my improving health, the worry lines left Tuck's face, his posture became more erect, his step lighter. Within six months after my operation, our lives had almost returned to normal.

How much more rested he looks, I thought one August morning as he leaned over to give me an absentminded kiss before heading out the door on his way to the office. After watching the gray-pinstriped figure disappear into the carport, I filled my mug with tea and carried it out onto the patio. *God, you are so good*! A feeling of peace and joy flooded my heart.

Sipping on the spicy tea, I wondered half-aloud, *What will we do today, Lord? I* need *to write letters—but surely You have something more exciting in store.*

My musing was interrupted by the ringing of the telephone in the family room. Taking my mug with me, I walked in and picked up the receiver. My "Hello" received no reply. Somehow the silence from the other end of the line seemed ominous.

"Hello?" I said it twice again before the caller replied. At first I didn't recognize the muffled voice—but as soon as she said "Aunt Helen," I knew it was Martha, my sister Millie's daughter. She was calling from her home in Myrtle Beach, South Carolina, where Millie was in the hospital.

"I have bad news," Martha told me between sobs. "Mother is dying. You all had better come down this weekend if you want to see her."

Terror gripped my heart. *Millie, dying? It can't be*!

"She was talking and laughing the first of the week," Martha continued a bit more calmly, "but now she's getting weaker and the doctor says it can't be much longer."

Now it was my end of the line that was silent. The mahogany clock on the antique bookcase chimed softly nine times while I tried to get my voice under control. *O God, You have promised not to put more on us than we can bear*. The thought brought instant comfort.

Finally I was able to thank Martha for phoning me, and to tell her that Tuck and I would come as soon as we possibly could. After hanging up the receiver, I sat in stunned silence, staring into the mug of tea I had put on the coffee table. *How normal it looks,* I thought, *just sitting there; yet my whole world has changed since I took my last sip from it. My sister is dying. I can't believe it.*

Millie had been fighting a good fight against breast cancer for well over twenty-three years, always winning every skirmish. *What happened, Lord?*

I longed for the release of tears, but no tears would come. Sunshine was still pouring through the windows, giving new brightness to the lemon-colored drapes—but a chill had come into the summer morning.

Dropping down on the sofa, I reached for the afghan that Friend Helen had knitted for me. Its warmth and softness comforted me as I lay down and pulled it up to my shoulders. Helen had worked on it while I was in the hospital, and as she knitted the brilliant golds and greens together, she prayed that it would bring blessings to me when I lay under it. How I needed those blessings now!

Since our parents died, Millie had been like a mother to my two younger sisters and me. She was the stalwart one, and our confidante. *What will the rest of us do without Millie to call on?*

My thoughts began to race, uncontrolled, as I fought against rising panic. *Lord, help me for Jesus' sake; I'm so weak . . . Lord, be merciful to me a sinner. (Wonder why I said that.) Though You slay me— O God . . . God . . . God! Help me! I know You aren't doing this—the enemy is pressing us sore. It's not Your highest will for our lives. You care for us. We believe in You. We trust You. Regardless. Even if we don't understand. Our hope is in Your wisdom and goodness. We rely on Your character. It is enough.*

Where is your God now? It was the voice of the tempter.

"Resist the devil, and he will flee from you." I welcomed the remembrance of that verse from James 4:7. Summoning my courage, I did as Jesus had done when He was tempted in the wilderness: I rebuked Satan and used the Sword of the Spirit (God's Word) to do battle with him.

"You will *not* discourage me, Satan," I said aloud. "My God lives!" My mind sought for a verse I could use against the tempter. It came readily: "Trust in the Lord with all thine heart; and lean not unto thine own understanding. In all thy ways acknowledge him, and he shall direct thy paths" (Proverbs 3:5,6). Then, "The Lord is good, a stronghold in the day of trouble; and He knows those who trust in Him" (Nahum 1:7 NKJV).

Yes, Lord, I trust You. It's all in Your hands.

I lost track of time while I was lying there talking to the Lord. Was it still morning or was it now early afternoon? Sitting up, I saw that the clock on the bookcase showed 12:15.

I must see Millie, I thought. *I* must. *I'll phone Tuck and see if he can make arrangements to drive me to Myrtle Beach tomorrow.*

Tuck's secretary was pleasant. "No, Mrs. Tucker, he just went out for lunch—but I'll leave a note on his desk for him to call you."

I put the telephone back into its cradle, fingering the silver filigree cover, zombie fashion. How Tuck had laughed when I installed "that nuisance" on the phone. He had never learned to like it. It's strange how our thoughts ramble when we're trying to put off thinking about the unendurable.

After napping fitfully for a few minutes, I drank some orange juice, then read my Bible and prayed while waiting for Tuck's call. No tears yet. *Lord, can't I even cry? Have I lost my ability to shed tears? . . . O Jesus, my good Friend, how You must love my sister! She is so true, so like You. Lord, please don't let her suffer.*

Calmer now, growing in faith, I began making plans for our trip. *If Tuck can cancel all his appointments for tomorrow,* I thought, *we'll go to see Millie. After we get there— Well, I'll trust God with everything.*

As always, God proved trustworthy. Tuck was eager to see Millie and was happy to drive me to Myrtle Beach. We left early the next morning.

When we entered the coastal highway—the last lap of our journey—seagulls swooped down close to the car, dipping their graceful wings toward us. They seemed to want us to follow them, to admire their beauty—but our thoughts were on what lay ahead. Tuck squeezed my hand lightly, as he often does when we are riding together. His reassuring touch comforted my saddened heart.

As we drew closer to our destination, I tried not to think of the familiar white walls and antiseptic odors that awaited us. The dread of returning to a hospital for the first time since my discharge added to the burden of my grief and anxiety for my sister. *Where is strength?*

I'm right here, came the unexpected reply. My heart welcomed the reminder of His presence. His words brought reassurance. Shifting my arm to a more comfortable position and tucking the small pillow under my elbow, I braced myself for the hundredth time.

God, I've almost forgotten to pray. Thank You for reminding me that You're here and that You'll be with us when we have to go into that hospital room.

Thoughts came and went. Millie and I had prayed over the phone every day for the past month. Sometimes she could only whisper; sometimes the nurses would hold the phone to her ear and she'd just listen. But we were always in the Spirit together, and we knew *He* was listening. Both of us drew strength from that daily contact. *If she's able to recognize me,* I thought, *I know she'll rejoice to see how well I'm looking. I pray she can.*

Realization that the car was slowing down put an end to my reverie. I looked out at the landscaped hospital grounds—once part of a magnificent plantation. Rows of stately palm trees, their fronds waving gently in the breeze, lined lush green lawns brilliant in summer sun. The hospital was an enormous colonial building, with rambling wings flowing out on both sides. *This should be a summer resort,* I thought. . . . *No, I'm glad it's a lovely-looking hospital instead, to shelter those who need it most—people like Millie. She loves God's whole creation so much! Flowers, sea, sky, people. She is filled with His love.*

My light jacket suddenly felt too warm around my shoulders. *Suppose I faint, get sick, cause some kind of scene. Lord, I cast myself fully on You. TAKE CARE OF ME.* I closed my eyes tight, and something like a faint whimper escaped my lips. Tuck placed his hand over mine.

When the car came to a stop, I knew it was time to go inside a hospital again; to see my sister, perhaps for the last time. The car door opened, and I heard Tuck's voice at the same time I felt his warm touch.

"Come on now, honey; hold onto my arm."

We made our way up the sloping driveway, to join Martha and her brother Andrew at the hospital entrance. Baby Daniel cooed sweetly in Martha's arms, totally unaware of the heavy hearts around him. Martha led the way through swinging glass doors and down a short hallway to Millie's room. On her door was a card proclaiming in small, beautifully printed letters, "JESUS CHRIST IS LORD!" How like Millie! My heart melted within me. Tuck was visibly moved.

He held fast to my arm as we stepped inside the room where my sister was lying on a familiar white bed. My saddened heart rejoiced when I saw her smiling at me. She recognized us! As I walked slowly toward the bed, I felt Tuck's arm against my shoulder, ready to steady me if I needed it.

I greeted Millie cheerfully—and although I couldn't understand her reply, I could see the love beaming out at me from her hazel eyes. Gently, I embraced her swollen body.

No one spoke for a long time; then I told her I loved her. She nodded that she knew. I asked forgiveness for hurtful words and deeds of long ago—once forgotten, now remembered. The smile on her face assured me I was already forgiven. Momentarily, I forgot Tuck, Andrew, and Martha—everyone but Millie. It was as if God had stopped the clock. My body, no longer tired, seemed light against her bedcovers. How long I stood, holding onto her, I don't know. Finally Tuck moved to my side.

"Millie, this is Tuck."

"I know," she said. Her smile was warm, triumphant, sure. "Soon I'll see Jesus." The words were spoken clearly.

"Yes, you will," I replied softly, kissing her cheek. I could tell that Millie was ready, even eager, to leave us and go to be with her husband John, our mother and daddy, and other family members who had gone on to heaven.

When the nurse left us alone with Millie—Martha, Tuck, Andrew, and me—we knew it was time to pray. As we stood beside the bed, I gave voice to the words that were formed inside me. Millie smiled and closed her eyes, seeming to savor each word. I knew they were words given by the Holy Spirit to bring comfort to the heart of one of His own.

When the prayer was finished, we stood still, letting Him have His way. Tuck was holding my hand in one of his, Millie's hand in the other. Silently, we both kissed her on the cheek. Then Tuck prayed a short prayer and whispered something in Millie's ear. Our visit was over.

As we left the room, I walked sideways, looking back as long as I could. I knew in my heart that this was the last time I would see Millie on earth—but I also knew it would be only a short time before all of us would be together in heaven forever. In spite of my sadness, my heart was at peace.

We met some other family members in the downstairs chapel and spent about an hour together—praying, talking, remembering. Then Martha and Andrew walked with us back to our car. As we kissed good-bye, we reassured each other of God's faithfulness and of Millie's love for us and for Jesus. Although Millie's two children were only in their twenties, I knew they would be all right. Like their mother, they possessed a strong faith.

Tuck stopped only once on the long trip home, to get some gas. Suppertime came and went unnoticed. I lay silently on the back seat of the automobile, grateful for the comfortable cushions to ease the ache in my tired body. I felt so weak and exhausted that I found myself wondering if I would be next. Was my time coming soon? If so, I hoped I would be as ready for God's call as Millie so obviously was.

I shivered as the enormous orange sun slid beneath the darkening horizon. As if by intuition, Tuck turned up the heater, bringing me welcome warmth. At last I was able to doze fitfully. As the miles passed, my thoughts—sometimes waking, sometimes sleeping—turned to Millie. Could it be that I would never touch her again, never hear her laugh at some silly joke? *What a wacky sense of humor that girl always had*! I remembered many things: our days of double-dating and going to dances together . . . the one brief, emotional period when we both dated the same boy in college. My memory darted here and there: schooldays . . . party dresses . . . hopscotch games . . . playing leapfrog on the preacher's lawn . . . dyeing Easter eggs . . . boys, boys, boys. *O dear God! How I miss her—already*! *She's only in her fifties, Lord.*

We arrived home about nine o'clock. At eight-thirty the next morning, we received a call saying Millie was gone.

Packing our clothes for the return journey to Myrtle Beach, I thought, *What a triumphant entry that must have been! Your daughter has finally come home, Jesus. You were there to meet her, and everything's all right with her and with us who are left behind. I can't imagine this world without her love in it; but Lord, You know best. That is enough.* At last the tears came, bringing release.

On a sunny summer afternoon, Millie was buried next to "Big John," her wonderful husband of many years. The cemetery was near the golden beach where they had loved to walk together. The gentle breezes and the palm trees seemed almost tropical—a setting inappropriate for a funeral. *But this is a coronation, not a funeral*! The thought thrilled me.

At the end of the service, after we had greeted those who lingered to speak to us, the members of Millie's "extended family" stood in a silent huddle, waiting for the last of our friends and neighbors to leave. Their presence, faithfulness, and acts of love had meant much to all of us—but now we longed to be together as a family, to talk, to share memories of Millie, to reassure and comfort each other. We looked forward to gathering at Andrew's house, where friends had prepared food to refresh us before we had to return to our separate homes.

I looked down into the wounded earth at the long silver box banked by brilliant flowers. I knew my sister had not attended this funeral. *She is not here; she is risen*! (See Matthew 28:6.) The precious words lifted my spirit. My heart sang to the whole world, "Rejoice in the Lord alway: and again I say, Rejoice" (Philippians 4:4).

Once again, as many times before, I had witnessed a strange phenomenon in this drama of going Home, in this Christian act of dying. That was the total absence of panic or fear in the one facing death. When God calls a child of His to come Home, that call seems to take precedence over every emotion, every personal desire. After quiet acceptance comes the longing to go, the looking forward to being with Him. The privilege of becoming inseparable from the Lord outweighs everything else.

My mind was occupied with these thoughts as my family and I walked quietly back to the grey limousines. *If the Lord should call* me *home soon,* I told myself, *He will have me ready and wanting to go. With the call comes the desire to answer.*

For today, however, "I shall not die, but live, and declare the works of the Lord" (Psalm 118:17). Indeed, I had already begun on that assignment.

26

Assignment from God

Soon after I came home from the hospital, the Lord had surprised me one morning with the announcement that we were going to tape-record the events of the past few weeks just as they had happened, day by day. I wondered where I would find the strength to talk into a tape recorder, and how I would be able to remember all that had taken place since that fateful New Year's Eve.

I should have known I could count on God's sufficient grace. Weak as I was, my voice remained strong for the taping sessions—at first fifteen minutes, then half an hour, and finally an hour or more. His strength was being made perfect in my weakness (see 2 Corinthians 12:9). And to my amazement, the Lord gave me almost total recall. Even past conversations came easily to mind as I began talking into the recorder under His direction.

It was exciting work. He would call me every day, usually after breakfast, to take the phone off the hook, settle down before Him with the recorder, and talk about the memories and ideas He gave me.

Soon I had amassed a large number of tapes. I had no idea what to do with them, so I just kept putting them into a shoe box. I knew that eventually the Lord would show me how they were to be used.

After each recording session, I spent many hours praying and meditating on the thoughts He gave me. I marveled at His grace and power in teaching, for each taping session brought fresh revelation and gave me food for thought.

Sometimes I wondered vaguely about God's purpose in having me do all this talking into a machine. Was He helping me get the stressful memories out into the open, so that He could purge them from my subconscious mind? (That thought recurred every time a taping session was emotionally difficult.) Or was He having me go over the lessons He had taught me in order to be sure they were firmly established in my mind and heart? No matter. He was in charge, and He knew what He was doing even if I didn't.

After I had been obediently recording for several weeks, He finally let me in on His plans for our tapes. Early one morning, I had finished a taping session and was settled back on the sofa, reading the Bible aloud to Him, when He called my name. *Helen, I've got a surprise for you. We're writing a book.* Although the words weren't spoken audibly, they were unmistakably clear to me.

I halfway rose from the sofa, laid my Bible face down on the coffee table, and pushed my bothersome reading glasses up to the top of my head so I could see clearly. "We're doing *what*? Say that *again*, Lord!"

You have been tape-recording your autobiography, He told me, *to bring hope and wholeness to people who will also be walking the road of adversity, through difficult trials and disappointments as you have walked. . . .*

"Lord, that's incredible! Are You *sure*?" For the second time, I spoke out loud, in total disbelief. Then I lay back on the sofa to ponder in amazement what God had just said to me.

Although the memory of His words stayed with me through the many recording sessions that followed, it never kept me from concentrating on His daily directions for each tape. We continued in the same simple, direct manner until one afternoon He told me we were through. I put the box of tapes away without ever listening to any of them. Just *recording* some of the traumatic events of my recent and remote past had produced enough emotional turmoil to last me forever.

After the tapes had stayed in a dresser drawer for several weeks, the Lord sent Friends Nancy, Jimi, Pat, Tom, and Sarah to let me know that they were to transcribe the tapes and help me get the material in shape to submit to a publisher.

Even after that job was done, however, I knew the book was still incomplete. I didn't know what was lacking, but there was definitely more to come. The manuscript went into a drawer, along with the shoe box full of tapes. In His time, I felt sure, Jesus would let me know what to do with it. For now, I must be content to wait. The wait would prove to be a long one.

Almost eight years after my surgery, Friend Sarah made a cryptic remark to me one day as we returned from a walk. "Helen," she said, "you have had many unusual encounters with God in the last few years."

We crossed my sun-streaked patio, pausing long enough to watch two quarrelsome bluejays squawking and pecking at each other over some sunflower seeds scattered around the birdbath. Their appetites seemed to be stimulated by the bright morning sunshine filtering down through the pine trees.

Sensing that my friend had something on her mind, I said, "Come on in, Sarah. Johnie, next door, gave me a box of exotic teas. Let's brew a pot."

"Sounds good," Sarah replied absently as we walked through the screened porch and entered the house. The water was soon boiling, and the pleasant aroma of tea floated through the kitchen. I cut two generous slices of Neighbor Margaret's lemon pound cake and slid them carefully onto bright blue dessert plates.

With steaming cups, Sarah and I sat facing each other on the twin sofas in the living room. Her blue eyes, usually sparkling with joy, were pensive, her expression solemn. I thought I knew my friend through and through, but at that moment she was different. "What's on your mind, old girl?" I asked between sips.

"The Lord has told me to ask you a very important question," Sarah replied, placing her untasted tea on the table. Knowing how much she loves tea, I was surprised. I've always thought Sarah would go to heaven with a china teacup in her hand.

"All right," I said. "What is it?"

"How has your life changed in the last eight years since your surgery?" Sarah spoke with deliberate emphasis on each word.

Sensing the importance of her question, I took my time in answering it. We sat in silence for several moments. *Lord,* I prayed deep down in my heart, *how* have *I changed*?

"Life seems more fragile, Sarah," I began tentatively. "It's not to be taken for granted, but to be enjoyed fully each moment. I used to think I'd be young, vigorous, and independent forever. Now I know better. Although my physical scars are now barely visible, it has taken a much longer time for God to dig down deep and reveal, then heal, the emotional scars I've carried, some even dating back to childhood. He has made great progress within me since I was sick."

I paused briefly, then continued. "My happiness is no longer dependent on circumstances, nor on people or happenings. I have learned that real joy comes only through trusting God completely and obeying Him implicitly. It's like the old hymn says, 'There's no other way to be happy in Jesus but to trust and obey.'

"The Bible tells us that Jesus came to *make us whole,* body, soul, and spirit—emotions and mind included—and whatever it takes to complete that wholeness, He will accomplish in us if we will only allow Him to do it."

I had started speaking slowly, but my thoughts were now flowing rapidly. "Do you remember the story about Jesus sending the disciples out on the lake when a storm was brewing? It's in Matthew 14, starting at verse 22."

I thrust a Bible into Sarah's hand and said, "What does it say?"

She read aloud: "And straightway Jesus constrained his disciples to get into a ship, and to go before him unto the other side."

"Read verse 24," I said.

"But the ship was now in the midst of the sea, tossed with waves: for the wind was contrary." When she had finished reading, Sarah looked at me expectantly.

"Don't you see it, Sarah? Jesus *sent* them out on the lake, even though He knew the storm was coming. He saw the crisis ahead, but he made them—'constrained them'—to get in the boat and leave Him behind. Why? They were His followers; yet He sent them alone into the very teeth of the storm.

"They were so busy rowing and trying to stay alive, they didn't have time to pray—but Jesus was praying for them. He knew where they were. Although they weren't aware of it, His eye was on them all the time. Exactly at the right moment, He walked out to them and calmed the seas, saving them. What was the result? Their faith in Him and their love for Him were mightily strengthened.

"He was preparing them for important days ahead—but at the time of their crisis they were totally unaware of His greater plans for their lives. In fact, they didn't even recognize *Him* when He drew near. Not until He spoke did they know who He was.

"That's how I look at my painful experience, Sarah. Jesus knew I had chosen to follow Him. He also knew where I was, and all the details of my circumstances, throughout the whole ordeal. Although He allowed me to experience the suffering, my crisis never escaped His gaze for one minute. Even when, just as the disciples did, I doubted Him, He brought me through victoriously for greater days ahead.

"What a wonderful God! His ways are perfect."

Sarah agreed with an elongated "Ah . . . *men.*"

I continued: "I've come to believe that it's impossible for a Christian to mature without some sort of testing sometime, somewhere along the way. God's highest purposes for us can be achieved only as we go with Him through the storms of life. When we can learn to trust Him and His ways of dealing with us, *even without understanding them,* He has won the victory in us—and He gives *us* the victory in our circumstances."

Sarah was in deep thought, teacup still forgotten. Impulsively, I went over and sat beside her.

"Sarah," I said, "*that's* the truth He wants me to share with you and with *every* believer. *That's* why He gave me the assignment of writing this book. He wants His children to realize that *His discipline is as much an evidence of His love for us as are the "goodies" He gives us.* He tells us that in His Word [Proverbs 3:11,12; Hebrews 12:5–11], but it wasn't until I was stripped of many of the things I thought were essential to my happiness—energy, travel, daily routine and activities—that I learned the deep truth of Hebrews 12:11. God's discipline *is* painful, and there were times when I felt helpless and alone in my trials—but when I turned to Jesus in trust and love, I found that He had never left me for a moment.

"That experience eight years ago was worth everything it cost me. I really lived out the truth of Romans 8:28. However, to answer your question, it has changed my life by bringing me infinitely closer to Jesus and greatly strengthening both my faith and my love for Him. I know Him now, not just as my Lord, my Savior, and my Healer, but as my never-changing, all-sufficient, always loving, ever-present-with-me, tried-and-found-totally-faithful Friend. I entered Room 321 as a child of God but emerged as a woman of God. Weeping may have endured for a night, but Joy came in the morning. I went through a very dark night, but—praise God—*Then, the Sun Came Up*!"

Sarah looked at me with a satisfied grin and said enthusiastically, "Now, let's have that cup of tea."

Appendix

SOME SCRIPTURE VERSES I FOUND HELPFUL

Thou, O Lord, art a shield for me; my glory, and the lifter up of mine head. (Psalms 3:3)

And they that know thy name will put their trust in thee; for thou, Lord, hast not forsaken them that seek thee. (Psalms 9:10)

The Lord is my helper; I will not be afraid. (Hebrews 13:6 NIV)

Let all those that seek thee rejoice and be glad in thee; let such as love thy salvation say continually, The Lord be magnified. (Psalms 40:16)

Yet the Lord will command his lovingkindness in the daytime, and in the night his song shall be with me, and my prayer unto the God of my life. (Psalms 42:8)

Why art thou cast down, O my soul? And why are thou disquieted within me? Hope thou in God: for I shall yet praise him, who is the health of my countenance, and my God. (Psalms 42:11)

The Lord will sustain him on his sickbed and restore him from his bed of illness. (Psalms 41:3 NIV)

Surely he [Jesus] hath borne our griefs, and carried our sorrows. . . . He was wounded for our transgressions, he was bruised for our iniquities; the chastisement of our peace was upon him; and with his stripes we are healed. (Isaiah 53:4, 5)

O Lord my God, I called to you for help and you healed me. (Psalms 30:2 NIV)

Trust in the Lord with all thine heart; and lean not unto thine own understanding. In all thy ways acknowledge him, and he shall direct thy paths. (Proverbs 3:5, 6)

Be strong and courageous. Do not be afraid or terrified because of them, for the Lord your God goes with you; he will never leave you nor forsake you. (Deuteronomy 31:6 NIV)

Yet I am always with you; you hold me by my right hand. (Psalms 73:23 NIV)

And surely I will be with you always, to the very end of the age. (Matthew 28:20 NIV)

For thus saith the Lord God, the Holy One of Israel: In returning and rest shall ye be saved; in quietness and in confidence shall be your strength. (Isaiah 30:15)

Then shall thy light break forth as the morning, and thine health shall spring forth speedily; and thy righteousness shall go before thee: the glory of the Lord shall be thy rereward. (Isaiah 58:8)

For I know the thoughts and plans that I have for you, says the Lord, thoughts and plans for welfare and peace, and not for evil, to give you hope in your final outcome. Then you will call upon Me, and you will come and pray to Me, and I will hear and heed you. Then you will seek Me, inquire for and require Me [as a vital necessity] and find Me; when you search for Me with all your heart, I will be found by you, says the Lord. . . . (Jeremiah 29:11–14a *AMPLIFIED*)

After reading this book, you may have begun thinking to yourself, *Yes, I would like to become a Christian. How do I do it?* Just read what follows. Jesus wrote it for you:

TO WHOMSOEVER IT MAY CONCERN:

For God so loved the world, that he gave his only begotten Son, that **whosoever** [that includes you] believeth in him should not perish, but have everlasting life. (John 3:16)

For there is no difference between the Jew and the Greek: for the same Lord over all is rich unto all that call upon him. For **whosoever** shall call upon the name of the Lord shall be saved. (Romans 10:12, 13)

As it is written, There is none righteous, no, not one. . . . For all have sinned, and come short of the glory of God. (Romans 3:10, 23)

. . . Christ died for our sins according to the scriptures; and that he was buried and that he rose again the third day according to the scriptures. (I Corinthians 15:3, 4)

If thou shalt confess with thy mouth the Lord Jesus, and shalt believe in thine heart that God hath raised him from the dead, thou shalt be saved. For with the heart man believeth unto righteousness, and with the mouth confession is made unto salvation. For the scripture saith, **Whosoever** believeth on him shall not be ashamed. (Romans 10:9–11)

Whosoever therefore shall confess me before men, him will I confess also before my Father which is in heaven. (Matthew 10:32)

PRAYER FOR WHOMSOEVER

Lord Jesus, be merciful to me a sinner. Forgive my sins. Save me. I receive You as my Lord and Savior. Thank You for hearing my prayer and saving me. In Jesus' name, Amen.

For speaking engagements, contact:

Helen Polston Tucker
c/o Star Books, Inc.
408 Pearson Street
Wilson, NC 27893

My Prayer for Health

Take this body, Lord,
    and mold it to Your liking.
Make it perform
    according to Your plan.
Conform it to Your will.

Cause it to be
    strong,
    workable,
    pliable
        under Your restraints;
    healthy,
    beautiful,
    controlled
        by Your will;
    living,
    moving, and
    having its being
            in You.

Cause it to function
    the way You created it to do—
        purposeful,
        reliable,
        normal
            in all its ways.

Let me see You
    in its life:
        acting at Your command,
        resting for Your purpose,
        waiting to hear Your Word.

Let this body be truly Yours,
    dedicated anew each morning
        not just to pleasure me but
    to give You satisfaction:
        its uttermost—my best.

So let the praises flow,
    its worship begin,
For creation has founded
    the body's true end:

    TO PRAISE YOU, MY GOD!